DUBLIN in BLOOMTIME

60 Shelbourne Roa.
Dublin

Dear Gogarty

I sent you back
the budget. I am still alive.
Here is a more reasonable
request. I am singing at a
garden-fête on Friday and
if you have a decent suit
before or a cricket shirt
send it or them. I am trying
to get an engagement in
the Kingstown Pavilion. Do
you know anyone there?
My idea for July & August
is this — to get Dolmetsch

to make me a lute and to
coast the south of England
from Falmouth to Margate
singing old English songs.
When are you leaving
Oxford? I wish I could see
it. I don't understand your
allusion. "Chamber Music"
is the title for the suite. I
suppose Jenny is leaving
in a day or so. I shall
call to say farewell and
adieu. Her letter did not
annoy me. The others did.
Enclose me lest you should
plume yourself. Elwood
is nearly cured. I have a
...

Langton — but you expel
her? I have no news
to report. Their Intensities
and their Bullockships
continue to flourish. His
Particular Intensity walks
now unencumbered. Hrabbly
is going for Greenwood Pim's
10th in CPI — desires to be
remembered to you. You
will not have me faithfully.
Adieu, then, Incertegant.

Stephen Dædalus.

3 June 1904

On 3rd June 1904, thirteen days before "Bloomsday", James Joyce wrote to his friend Gogarty asking for the loan of a "decent suit" or a "cricket shirt" so he could sing at a garden-fête. He signed the letter "Stephen Daedalus".

DUBLIN in BLOOMTIME

THE CITY JAMES JOYCE KNEW

BY CYRIL PEARL

A Studio Book · THE VIKING PRESS · New York

Copyright © 1969 by Cyril Pearl
All rights reserved

Published in 1969 by The Viking Press, Inc.
625 Madison Avenue, New York, N.Y. 10022

Library of Congress catalog card number: 69–17971

Printed and bound in Great Britain by
Jarrold & Sons Ltd, Norwich

ACKNOWLEDGMENTS

This book could not have been made without the
gracious assistance of Mr Patrick Henchy, Director
of the National Library, Dublin, and his enthusiastic
staff, and of Miss Vivian Beale, the charming custodian
of the Martello Tower at Sandycove.
All the photographs are from the archives of the
National Library.

Book designed by Francis J. Broadhurst

DUBLIN IN BLOOMTIME

*Dublin's finest building, the
Customs House, was designed by
James Gandon, an English
architect of Huguenot parentage,
and built between 1781 and 1791.* ▶

"So far no one has committed the mind of our Dubliners to the pages of a book," lamented a writer in the *Dubliner* early in 1905. "Novelist—in Dublin you will find material sufficient for twenty masterpieces." He was not to know that a twenty-eight-year-old Dubliner of genius, self-exiled to Europe, was then committing not only the mind of the Dubliner but the fabric, the essence, the spirit of Dublin itself, to a book—the first of four in which his native city was commemorated.

James Joyce's Dublin is an eternal city, preserved against time and change by his unchanging love for it. "There was an English Queen who said that when she died the word 'Calais' would be written on her heart. 'Dublin' will be found on mine," Joyce told Hannah Sheehy-Skeffington, the wife of one of his best friends. And he used to boast that if Dublin were destroyed it could be reconstructed from his books. "In his books," says his most distinguished biographer, Richard Ellmann, "his care for insuring the accuracy of unimportant details argues a love for them which may seem immoderate even in our documentary age."

Joyce left Dublin in 1904, when he was twenty-two, and except for two brief visits, never saw it again. But in a sense he never left the city he had grown up in. Its noble buildings and ignoble slums, its churches and brothels, its pub-keepers, its writers and eccentrics, were fixed immutably in his memory. He treasured even the trivia of Dublin, what he called its "street furniture", its advertisements and its shopfronts. As an exile in Paris, he took pride in his ability to list the shops of Talbot Street—a shabby, unimportant street that runs from where the Nelson Pillar once stood to Amiens Street station—in order, down one side and up the other. And he stimulated his acute "consciousness of place" by studying Dublin directories, newspapers, and periodicals.

When he was discussing the publication of *Dubliners* with Grant Richards, the publisher—it was accepted in 1906 but, because of objections to some passages, not published till 1914—Joyce wrote to Richards that Dublin "has been a capital of Europe for thousands of years. . . . Moreover . . . the expression 'Dubliner' seems to me to have some meaning, and I doubt whether the same can be said for such words as 'Londoner' and 'Parisian'."

Years later he said to the Irish poet Austin Clarke, who called on him in Paris: "Dublin is the nearest city to the Continent. Places here in Paris on a Saturday night are like Capel Street and Thomas Street. There are the same joy and excitement, as though bargaining for Sunday's dinner was a holiday." He saw Dublin as

Stephen's Green north, with a D.B.C. tea-room. "We call it D.B.C.," says Buck Mulligan, "because they have damn bad cakes." None the less, he orders cakes with his mélange, *scones and butter.*

a city "old enough to be considered as a representative European capital: small enough to be viewed as whole".

Much of Dublin was destroyed during the Easter Rising, the War of Independence, and the Civil War. More recently, "developers"—a current euphemism for despoilers—have continued the sack of the city. Yet, surprisingly, much of Joyce's Dublin, the Dublin of "Bloomtime", remains. Leopold Bloom's own house, No. 7 Eccles Street, empty and decrepit, was de-molished in 1967. (The area through which he entered early in the morning of 17th June 1904 had become a repository for rusty tin cans and dead cats, and the roof was falling in.) But across the road, Larry O'Rourke's pub is still on the corner of Dorset Street ("From the cellar grating floated up the flabby gush of porter. Through the open doorway the bar squirted out whiffs of ginger, teadust, biscuitmush"), though façade and licensee have changed. There is still a chemist shop, with a weighing-machine outside, at the

Hamilton Long's "Compounding Establishment" in Grafton Street, "founded in the year of the flood".

corner of Dorset and Great Frederick streets, where Bloom weighed himself ("eleven stone four pounds") on 12th May 1904, and three golden balls still proclaim a pawnshop at 52 Dawson Street nearby. Many of the shops named in *Ulysses* remain in business— among them, Switzers, Clery's, Hely's, and Brown Thomas. Combridge's corner with its ornate iron-lace shopfront has not changed since Mr Bloom passed it on his way to the Burton restaurant; Cantrell and Cochrane continue to bottle mineral waters in Nassau Place, though they no longer boast, as they did in 1904, "Purveyors to H.R.H. The Prince of Wales"; and Hamilton Long's, the Grafton Street chemists, who, according to Bloom, were "founded in the year of the flood", still timelessly proclaim their premises to be a "Compounding Establishment".

O'Connell (formerly Carlisle) Bridge, also designed by Gandon, was widened and flattened in 1880. Today it is as wide as it is long.

1 W.—Tyrone-street, Lr.

From Gardiner-street, Lower, to Buckingham-street, Lower.

P. St. Thomas.—North Dock W.

1 and 2 Tenements,	9l., 2l.
3 Ruins,	

.... *here Mabbot-lane intersects*..........

4 Tenements,	20l.
5 Hayes, Mrs.	18l.
6 Jones, Mrs.	18l.
7 & 7½ Thompson, W. and P. stores,	6l. and 8l.
8 Hayes, J., dealer and coal store	8l.
9 Barnett, Mr. John,	14l.
10 M'Donald, A. dairy,	14l.
11 M'Mahon, Edwd. prov. dealer,	18l.

... .*here Mabbot-street intersects*........

12 Vacant,	10l.
13 & 14 St. Patrick's Schools—Andrew Scully, head master,	14l. 15s.
15 Redhouse, W. J. dairy,	15l.
16 & 17 Tenements,	8l., 9l.
18 Holmes, William J. restaurant	9l.
19 Tenements,	6l.
20 Vacant,	11l. 10s.
21 Kavanagh, Patk. groc. & vint.— res. 41 North Strand-road,	15l.

.........*here Elliott-place intersects*........

22 Vacant	
23 Vacant,	8l.
24 Vacant,	9l.
25 Tenements,	8l. 10s.
26 Brady, Patrick, grocer, &c.	16l. 10s.

. .....*here Faithful-place intersects*. .....

27, 28 & 29 Ruins,	
30 and 31 Tenements,	7l. 10s. 11l.
32 and 33 Davis, Miss	
34 and 35 Ruins	
36 & 37 Tenements,	11l. and 10l.
38 and 39 Smyth, Mrs.	10l. and 11l.
40 and 41 Tenements,	each 13l.

..........*here Uxbridge intersects*........ ..

42 to 44 Tenements,	4l.,12l. 10s., 10l.
45 Farrell, Patrick, prov. dealer,	11l.
46 and 47 Tenements,	13l. 10s. & 9l.
48 Brady, Pk. grocer & spirit dlr.	15l.

.........*here Beaver-street intersects*..... ..

49 Vacant,	4l.
50 to 53 Tenements,	9l. each
54 Synnott, Joseph J. horse dealer,	10l.
55 to 57 Tenements,	8l.

..*here Buckingham-st. Lower, intersects*

58 and 59 Forbes, Alexander, brass foundry	
60 to 65 Tenements,	each 11l.
66 Tenements,	11l.
67 Tenements,	11l.
68 to 80 St. Mary's Penitent Retreat	
81 Callan, Miss,	6l.
82 Cohen, Mrs.	20l.
83 Arnott, Mrs.	12l.
84 Brooker, Mrs.	20l.
85 Mack, Mrs. Annie	20l.
86 to 88 Tenements,	20l., 20l., 8l.
89 Tenements,	12l.

.......*here Byrne's-square intersects*..... ..

90 Tenements,	12l.
91 Reilly, Mrs. dairy,	10l.
92 Vacant,	5l.
93 and 94 Tenements,	8l. 10s.
95 Building ground	
96 and 97 Tenements,	5l., 6l.

2 S.—Trin

From College-green

P. St. Andrew.—

The West End C Star Buildings,

2 The National Cash —W. E. Holdo

3 Dillon, Michael, Cratloe, Merric

„ Dillon, Frank, Cratloe, Merric

„ Dillon, William res. Cratloe,

4 Stewart, T. E. merchant tail

„ O'Reilly, the M and Ennis

5 Bulger, D. S. and ment stockbr Liverpool and Insurance Co.

„ Kirwan, P. J. broker—res. Ailesbury-roa

6 O'Connell, B. law and typev

„ Bentley and C stockbrokers

„ Bentley, Geo. F. stockbroker — terrace, Monk

„ Carlyle, Rober stockbroker— Ailesbury-roa

7 Wilson, Samu

„ Smith, Willia

8 Willman Brot &c.

„ Smith, Lewis

„ Aitkin, Rober Londonderry

„ Alexander, Jos Londonderry

„ O'Donnell, Ja Londonderry

„ Alexander, Jc Belfast

„ Galway and Be Belfast

„ Galway, Jame Belfast

„ M'Caughey an Ballymena

„ M'Caughey, Ballymena

„ Turnbull, N. H

„ Wilson, J. G. N

„ Johnston, J. and Omagh

„ Currie, John Ballymena

„ Wilson, John 60 Donegall-

„ Tomb, John Kilrea

„ Anderson and Coleraine

„ O'Doherty, Ja Londonderry

„ Dunford, Da Waterford

„ Cooney, A. Enniskillen

„ Nooney, P. J.

„ O'Donovan, P Clonakilty

„ Reid, John Kei and Londond

In 1904, the year in which *Ulysses* is set, Joyce was an Angry Young Man, bored, frustrated, ambitious, egotistical, and defiant. Drinking and whoring, he lay waste his powers. "He gets drunk in a regular way, by lounging from one public-house to another," his brother Stanislaus noted in his diary in September. "He tried it first as an experience, for the want of something more interesting to do." And his younger brother, Charlie, was an eager disciple in debauchery. "Charlie has been in gaol for drunkenness," Stanislaus recorded in April. "The fine was paid after four days and he was released. . . . He was something of a hero after this exploit, and lately has been obviously emulating James in drinking and whoring. He has slept three nights running with a whore in Tyrone Street." According to Stanislaus, Joyce, as well as working on the stories afterwards published as *Dubliners*, was writing a series of studies on syphilitic contagion, "tracing practically everything to it". There were ample facilities for field-work; prostitution was one of Dublin's few flourishing industries. There are no statistics, but in 1904, 586 prostitutes were arrested in Dublin, compared with 4,333 in London. Dublin's population was about 400,000 and London's about 7,000,000. The ratio of arrested prostitutes to population was therefore more than twice as high in Dublin as in London. Besides its streetwalkers, subject to arrest for soliciting, Dublin had, unlike London, a considerable population of whores who functioned lawfully in brothels.

"Dublin seems to form an exception to the usual practice in the United Kingdom. In that city police permit open brothels confined to one area, but carried on more openly than in the South of Europe or even Algiers," said the *Encyclopaedia Britannica*. The area comprised many city blocks around the former Mecklenburgh Street, on land mostly belonging to the estate of the Earl of Blessington. In *Ulysses*, Joyce calls this district "Nighttown", but the popular Dublin name for it was "Monto", because Montgomery Street bordered it. In 1887, Mecklenburgh Street was renamed Tyrone Street, and later Railway Street, to purge it of its unholy associations. (It was embarrassingly close to the Catholic Pro-Cathedral in Marlborough Street.) Today most of Monto has vanished in a waste of parking-lots and corporation flats; but Mabbot Lane, running from Talbot Street to Railway Street, survives.

Monto was once a modish residential district. Mecklenburgh Street in the eighteenth century was inhabitated by the aristocracy, and in the early part of the nineteenth century by wealthy professional men.

This photograph of Joyce in 1904 aged 22 was taken by his University College friend Constantine P. Curran. When Joyce was asked what he was thinking at the time, he said: "I was wondering would he lend me five shillings."

Oliver St John Gogarty (the "stately, plump Buck Mulligan" of Ulysses*) was four years younger than Joyce, whom he met while both were waiting for books at Dublin's National Library one night in 1903. Gogarty taught Joyce to drink.*

The famous Misses Gunning, who became, respectively, the Duchess of Hamilton and the Countess of Coventry, were born in Mecklenburgh Street, not far from where the infamous Bella Cohen and Mrs Mack later held court. There were forty-three tenement houses in Mecklenburgh Street in 1850, and seventy-five in 1900. A similar decline took place in Marlborough Street, where the Marquis of Waterford once had his mansion, Tyrone House, with the Viscount Avonmore as neighbour.

There were sharp class distinctions in Monto. The most select part was the upper end of Tyrone Street, where the Georgian houses retained some of their elegance and the whores wore fashionable evening dress and were visited regularly by their couturier. Less fastidious were their sisters at the lower end, and in Mabbot Street and Faithful Place, who wore only raincoats which they flicked open occasionally to stimulate trade. In these humbler establishments, "coshes" of lead pipe were often concealed behind the gaudy religious pictures that brightened the walls.

One of the most eminent of the high-class madams, Meg Arnot, lived in luxury in Mount Merrion, kept her daughter at an expensive English convent school, and ritualistically drove her girls in a landau down Grafton Street every Saturday to exhibit them to the gentry. Another esteemed hostess was Bella Cohen, of 82 Tyrone Street, in whose pleasure-dome much of the "Circe" scene in *Ulysses* takes place. Joyce describes her with brutal precision: "She is dressed in a threequarter ivory gown, fringed round the hem with tasselled selvedge, and cools herself, flirting a black horn fan. . . . On her left hand are wedding and keeper rings. Her eyes are deeply carboned. She has a sprouting moustache. Her olive face is heavy, slightly sweated and fullnosed, with orangetainted nostrils. She has large pendant beryl eardrops" and "falcon" eyes that "glitter".

Oliver Gogarty is no more flattering about Mrs Cohen's equally well-known neighbour, Mrs Mack, who had two places of business—numbers 85 and 90. "Is this Mrs Mack's?" Bloom asks Zoe Higgins, "a young whore in a sapphire slip, closed with three bronze buckles, a slim black velvet fillet round her throat", and Zoe answers, "No, eightyone. Mrs Cohen's. You might go farther and fare worse." Gogarty describes Mrs Mack's "brick-red face, on which avarice was written

The soldiery at play on Killiney Strand.

like a hieroglyph, and a laugh like a guffaw in hell."
She used to discuss her clientele frankly with him:
"Them incorporated accountants make me sick. Never
come here decent and honest; but always with ex-
cuses."

One of Bella Cohen's young ladies in *Ulysses*, "a
bony pallid whore in navy costume, doeskin gloves
rolled back from a coral wristlet, a chain purse in her
hand", whose hair, "red with henna", glows under her
sailor hat, has been identified by Professor Ellmann as
Becky Cooper, "probably the best-known among
Dublin prostitutes from the beginning of the century
until the twenties". She was noted for her generosity,
often bestowing gifts of money or clothes on young
clients whom she liked, and a popular song acclaimed
her gratefully:

> *Italy's maids are fair to see*
> *And France's maids are willing*
> *But less expensive, 'tis to me,*
> *Becky's for a shilling.*

As a young medical student, Gogarty visited the
kips "decent and honest" and made many verses about
them. Of his illustrious whoring companion he wrote:

> *There is a young fellow named Joyce*
> *Possessed of a sweet tenor voice,*
> *He goes down to the kips*
> *With a song on his lips,*
> *And biddeth the harlots rejoice.*

In later years, as a fashionable Dublin doctor,
Gogarty sang the passing of the kips in a nostalgic
ballade:

> *Where are the great kip Bullies gone,*
> *The Bookies and outrageous Whores*
> *Whom we so gaily rode upon,*
> *When youth was mine and youth was yours:*
> *Tyrone Street of the crowded doors*
> *And Faithful Place so infidel?*
> *Fresh Nellie's gone and Mrs Mack.*
> *May Oblong's gone and Number Five*
> *Where you could get so good a back*
> *And drinks were so superlative.*

But Gogarty's most memorable brothel-inspired

verse appeared anonymously during the Boer War in Dublin's leading—and most snobbish—society magazine. Published as a rapturous "Ode to Welcome" to heroic Irish regiments returning from South Africa, it read:

The Gallant Irish yeoman,
Home from the war has come
Each victory gained o'er foeman,
Why should our bards be dumb?

How shall we sing their praises
Or glory in their deeds?
Renowned their worth amazes,
Empire their prowess needs.

So to Old Ireland's hearts and homes
We welcome now our own brave boys
In cot and hall; 'neath lordly domes
Love's heroes share once more our joys.

Love is the Lord of all just now,
Be he the husband, lover, son,
Each dauntless soul recalls the vow
By which not fame, but love was won.

United now in fond embrace
Salute with joy each well-loved face,
Yeoman, in women's hearts you hold the place.

There was an unprecedented demand for the magazine when the intelligence was flashed through Dublin pubs and clubs that the initial letters of each line spelled out a less rapturous acrostic: THE WHORES WILL BE BUSY. Licentious soldiery were in fact one of the mainstays of the brothels and the itinerant whores. Each year the August Horse Show brought a rush of business to Monto, when eager British officers came to Dublin to see the horses and found time to see the whores as well. The well-bred ladies of Tyrone Street punctiliously sent their cards in to the Mess, and drove their little pony traps to the races, in the tradition of the pretty Victorian "horsebreakers", Skittles, Agnes Willoughby, and Mabel Gray. The officers returned the compliment by driving back to Monto in fleets of Dublin cabs.

About 5,000 soldiers, English and Irish, were stationed in Dublin. The "tommies" patronized the cheaper houses in Tyrone Street, and the cheaper whores in Sackville—now O'Connell—Street, where their unrestrained behaviour, especially on Sunday nights, evoked a protest from the Dublin Corporation. In June 1904 it called on the British authorities "to abate the nuisance caused by the British soldiers in the streets of the capital". Mr Corrigan, speaking in favour of the resolution, said he was a loyal man, but "neither in Paris, Port Said, Cairo, nor Bombay, had he witnessed such scenes".

When the British Government rejected the protest, which Maud Gonne endorsed, Arthur Griffith's *United Irishman* commented bitterly: "The British Government has officially announced that . . . it intends to take no steps to prevent the continuance of scenes which have earned for Dublin abroad the reputation of being one of the most immoral cities in the world. . . . That is what we expected it to announce. . . . Dublin is nicknamed in the British army 'the soldiers' Paradise' because in no city in Great Britain or in any part of the British Empire is such latitude permitted to the soldiery as in Dublin."

Mr Bloom, strolling out of Westland Row post-office guiltily with a letter from Martha Clifford in his pocket, encounters a grenadier in bearskin cap and hackle plume and moralizes: "Redcoats. Too showy. That must be why the women go after them. Uniform . . . Maud Gonne's letter about taking them off O'Connell street at night: disgrace to our Irish capital. Griffith's paper is on the same tack now: an army rotten with venereal disease: overseas or halfseasover empire."

In his later years Gogarty had an ingenious scheme "to reduce the enormity of both these outrages on good taste and good living: banks and brothels". It was to turn the banks into brothels and the brothels into banks. He explains it in his spirited book of reminiscences, *As I Was Going Down Sackville Street.* At first there would just be an exchange of staffs between brothels and banks. But all future banks would be placed in Tyrone Street; "each next door to a kip, in the following order":

Bank of Ireland, Mrs Mack's; Teasey Ward's, Belfast Bank; Munster and Leinster, Liverpool Kate's; Piano Mary's, Provincial Bank; Mrs Hayes' next to the Royal and May Oblong's next to the Northern Bank. . . . Instead of having the most squalid, foetid and miserable stews in Europe, Dublin would find itself without a kip of any kind except those "in process of alteration" by the bankers. Baths would be introduced; and with the sentiment of the Georgian period preserved . . . the kips would be exemplary specimens of good and careful enterprise, while the banks would be efficient houses of correction for pretentiousness and display.

"Redcoats. Too showy. That must be why the women go after them."

Sandymount Green, three miles from Nelson's Pillar.

The Martello Tower at Sandymount, where Joyce lived from 9th September to 19th September 1904.

The Martello Tower at Sandymount, a village on the southern shore of Dublin Bay, where Joyce lived briefly with Oliver Gogarty in 1904, and in which the opening scene of *Ulysses* is set ("Stately, plump Buck Mulligan came from the stairhead . . ."), was one of nine or ten stone fortresses built round the Irish coast from Bray to Dublin as a defence against Napoleonic invasion. "The building of the Martello Towers . . . proceeds with unexampled despatch," says a contemporary report. "They are in general forty feet in diameter, precisely circular, and built of hewn granite closely jointed. Some are already thirty feet high, and exhibit proofs of the most admirable masonry." The walls were nine feet thick, there was a large flagged

room with a fireplace—the "gloomy domed living-room" of *Ulysses*—entered by an iron ladder staircase about twenty feet from the ground, and three small rooms, one a copper-sheathed powder magazine, below. A small spiral staircase led from the main room to the gun-rest on the parapet.

The origin of the name "Martello" is obscure. Gogarty derives it from "mallet", because, he says, the tower was shaped like a sculptor's mallet. Others say it came from the name of the Corsican who designed the towers, or from Mortella Bay in Corsica, where the English first encountered such a tower, in 1794.

In his *Rambles in Erin*, Mr William Bulfin describes a visit to the tower that he made, cycling with a friend,

16

one Sunday morning in 1904:

My Comrade . . . said casually that there were two men living in the tower . . . who were creating a sensation in the neighbourhood. . . . The poet was a wayward kind of genius, who talked in a captivating manner, with a keen grim humour. . . . The other poet listened in silence, and when we went on the roof he disposed himself restfully to drink in the glory of the sunshine. . . . We looked northward to where the lazy smoke lay on the Liffey's banks, and southward, over the roofs and gardens and parks to the grey peak of Killiney, and then westward and inland to the blue mountains.

Joyce and Gogarty paid eight pounds a year rent to the Secretary of State of War. The official receipt is preserved among exhibits in the living-room of the tower, now a Joyce museum. After Joyce left, Gogarty shared the tower with Seamus O'Sullivan and Arthur Griffith.

A Dublin United Tramways Company guidebook of 1904 describes the twenty-minute journey from the Nelson Pillar to Sandymount, a distance of three miles:

The Cars start from Nelson's Pillar, and pass along the east side of Lower Sackville Street across O'Connell Bridge, and through D'Olier Street to Brunswick Street into which they turn to the left and continuing through its whole length, passing Westland Row on the right, cross the new Swing Bridge, over the Canal Dock into Ringsend-road; the Central Power Station of the Company being on the left, conspicuous by its two very tall chimney-shafts and at which the whole of the electric current required in the working of the system is generated; they pass thence over the Ringsend Bridge (close to the homes of several Dublin Rowing Clubs), through the essentially fishing village of Ringsend and Irishtown and Sandymount Road to Sandymount village through the Strand Road skirting the seashore to the Martello Tower, where they stop.

"The tramcar is the social confessional of Dublin,"

17

wrote Tom Kettle, the brilliant young writer who was killed in World War I. "Sixpence prudently spent on fares will provide you with a liberal education." Dublin's tramway system was one of the best in the world; horse trams, introduced in 1872, had been replaced in 1901 by double-deck electric trams. Austin Clarke recalls the magic they had for him as a child: "As the front of them was open, the drivers could be seen moving their brass levers controlling the wonderful current of electricity which sometimes spluttered in bad temper from the top of the trolley: on wet days, they glistened in tarpaulins as they slowed down their light-ning, the rain coursing down their cheeks, thickening their whiskers and streaming over their leather gloves." There is poetry even in their destinations, as Joyce invokes them: "Before Nelson's Pillar trams slowed, shunted, changed trolley, started for Blackrock, Kingstown and Dalkey, Clonskea, Rathgar and Terenure, Palmerston park and upper Rathmines, Sandymount Green, Rathmines, Ringsend and Sandymount Tower, Harold's Cross." The electric trams disappeared in 1949, replaced by undistinguished buses, and Nelson's Pillar disappeared in 1966, blown up by unidentified hooligans.

Traffic jam in Grafton Street. ▶

"I wandered along towards Grafton Street where I stood for a long time leaning against a lamppost, smoking," Joyce wrote to his future wife, Nora Barnacle, in August 1904. "The street was full of a life which I have poured a stream of my youth upon."

Oliver St John Gogarty thought that the three best streets in Dublin were Grafton, Dawson, and Kildare, each a little over a hundred yards in length, each running from St Stephen's Green to Trinity College. It is in Grafton Street, "gay with housed awnings", that Mr Bloom lingers, his senses lured by its abundant life and colour: "Muslin prints, silk, dames and dowagers, jingle of harnesses, hoofthuds lowringing in the baking causeway." He dallies appreciatively by the windows of Brown Thomas; "Cascades of ribbons: Flimsy China silks. A tilted urn poured from its mouth a flood of bloodhued poplin. . . . Gleaming silks, petticoats on slim brass rails, rays of flat silk stockings."

"Blazes" Boylan stops at Thornton's, in Grafton Street, to buy some fat pears and "ripe shamefaced peaches" for Molly Bloom. Mr Thornton was Dublin's leading fruiterer; as he modestly advertised:

To say that Mr Thornton is fruit merchant and florist by special warrants to His Majesty the King, His Excellency the Lord Lieutenant, His Royal Highness the Prince of Wales, and His Royal High-

*Thornton's fruit shop,
in Grafton Street.*

ness the Duke of Connaught, is the best indication
of the extent and high-class quality of the business
which he carries on at 63 Grafton Street. The stock
includes hothouse pineapples, Muscatel grapes,
Jersey pears, oranges, custard apples, etc., asparagus,
seakale, new potatoes, hothouse French beans,
salads, etc., orchids, lily of the valley, carnations,
Harris and arum lilies, chrysanthemums, coloured
roses, mistletoe, etc. Mr Thornton is also agent in
Dublin for Fuller's celebrated sweets and confectionery. All articles in which the establishment deals
are beautifully made up and prices will be found
very reasonable.

Mr Thornton's admirable establishment is no more,
but Piggot's, where Joyce bought (or borrowed
briefly) on time payment a grand piano to practise
songs for the 1904 Feis Coil, are still selling grand
pianos—as well as electric guitars—in their Grafton
Street warehouse. Joyce won a medal in the Feis Coil,
Dublin's annual musical festival, popularly known as
the "Fish Coil", and three months later sang in the
Antient Concert Rooms on the same programme as
John McCormack.

The Dublin of Bloomtime was a very musical city.
"Its old men and young men, its women and girls
abounded in talk of operas and musical plays," says
Mary Colum. In many houses entertainment meant
music, singing, cakes and tea, and opera societies
flourished. One was supported by Mr Cochrane, the
mineral-water manufacturer, who used to sing in its
regular performances of *Faust*, *The Bohemian Girl*,
and *The Lily of Killarney*.

In the 1901 census, Dublin had 233 female and 169
male music-teachers.

20   *Grafton Street, "gay with housed awnings".* ▶

In the explosive political climate of Ireland, statues of celebrities have always had a precarious existence, particularly celebrities on horseback, perhaps because of their greater fragility.

King Billy's statue in College Green (the lead statue of William III, commemorating the defeat of James II at the Battle of the Boyne) was formally honoured by Protestants twice a year—on the anniversary of the battle, and on the King's birthday—and informally dishonoured by Catholics at any odd time when no one was looking. As a Dublin guide-book put it, "It has been insulted, mutilated and blown up so many times that the original figure, never particularly graceful, is now a battered wreck, pieced and patched together like an old worn-out garment." It was rebuilt so often that the raised left leg was about a foot longer than the right. When the statue was again blown up in 1929 it was beyond plastic surgery. The fragments were collected and melted down.

As a young man, Joyce amused himself by suggesting new inscriptions for Dublin's statues. "Now, where did I put that stud?" for Bishop Plunket in Kildare Street, and "Oh, I know", for Tom Moore in College Green. Tommy Moore still wags his "roguish finger" above a public lavatory, a conjunction which sets Bloom thinking: "They did right to put him up over a urinal: meeting of the waters."

Bishop Plunket: "Now where did I put that stud?"

Thomas Moore: "Oh, I know."

"The poets have ceased to sing, the fiddling, the piping and the dancing at the cross-roads have gone; the hurling has died out," lamented Arthur Griffith in his *United Irishman* a few days before Bloomsday—16th June 1904, the day on which the action of *Ulysses* takes place. "The so-called education introduced by England has stamped out the native culture; it has half-taught the people English . . . it has given them at best *Answers*, *Tit-Bits* and the *Freeman's Journal*." Joyce used to say that the *United Irishman*, a vigorous voice of Irish nationalism, was the only paper in Dublin worth reading, but Griffith was not quite accurate in his diagnosis of its cultural health. There was much creative activity in Dublin at the time. Yeats, Moore, Synge, and Lady Gregory were writing, the Abbey Theatre was taking shape, Constance Gore Booth and George Russell ("A.E.") were painting, and Russell, a poet as well as a painter, was encouraging many young writers, including Joyce. As Joyce's biographer, Richard Ellmann, says: "The Irish literary movement, fostered by Standish O'Grady, John O'Leary, Yeats, Douglas Hyde, and others, had made Dublin an intellectual centre."

Joyce's first published short story appeared in Russell's agricultural journal, the *Irish Homestead*, on 13th August 1904. No writer of genius has ever made a more incongruous début. Joyce called the *Irish Homestead* "the pig's paper"; his story, an embryonic version of "The Sisters", by-lined "Stephen Daedalus", is mentioned last in a list of contents that includes articles on Duck Rearing, Cold Sweets, and Bee-Keeping As An Occupation For Women. The first page of the story is decorated with an advertisement for Cantrell and Cochrane's Mineral Waters, the second with an advertisement for Cream Separators, Milk Pumps, and Refrigerating Machines. Joyce received a sovereign for this story, and the same payment for two published subsequently, "Eveline" (10th September) and "After the Race" (17th December). The *Irish Homestead* was killed when a priest succeeded in a libel action against it.

The *United Irishman* was a stern custodian of Dublin's morals. Even the mutescope machines—forerunners of the cinema—in which you turned a crank and saw a succession of photographs—at the Royal Dublin Society's Spring Show of 1904, incurred its displeasure. Quoting titles such as "Mixed Bathing", "Love in the Suburbs", "Changing the Bather's Clothes", "The Lovers were having a Good Time but the Wife came on the Scene", "How Minnie got her Leg pulled", and "Married Women will appreciate This", it castigated "the prurient creatures" who, attracted by these provocative titles, dropped their pennies in the slots.

The *United Irishman* also disapproved strongly of a recent performance in the Queen's Theatre:

> One of the items was a song sung by a woman who wore a skirt which reached only to her knees, and who concluded her part of the programme by turning a somersault, about a visit to Paris and the "can-can", the chorus of which began "Look at the lace, boys", the singer illustrating the song by hitching up her skirt. And the chief attraction was a sketch in which semi-nude women, posing for a pseudo-artist, were supposed to be peered at from behind a screen by men who paid the pseudo-artist £10 each for the privilege.

Freeman's Journal *announces the concert on 27th August 1904, in which Joyce shared the platform with John McCormack. "Mr Joyce possesses a light tenor voice, which he is inclined to force on the high notes . . ." wrote a critic. "One of his selections, 'Down by the Sally Gardens', suited his method best; and, as an encore, he tenderly gave 'My Love Was Born in the North Countree', a short and sweet piece." Joyce also gave "a pathetic rendering" of "The Croppy Boy".*

O, King of Glory, is it not a great change
  Since I was a young man, long, long ago?
When the heat of the sun made my face glow
  As I cut the grass, on a fine cloudless day;
Fair girls laughing
  All through the field raking hay,
Merry in the fragrant morning,
  And the sound of their voices like music in the air.

The bees were after the honey,
  Taking it to their nests among the hay,
Flying against us nimbly and merrily,
  And disappearing from sight with small keen buzz.
And the butterflies on the thistles,
  And on the meadow daisies, and from flower to flower,
On light wing lying and rising up,
  Moving through the air—they were fine.

The blackbird and the thrush were in the small nut wood,
  Making sweet music like the songs of the bards,
And the sprightly lark with a song in her little mouth
  Poising herself in the air aloft.
The beautiful thrush was on top of the branch,
  His throat stretched out in melodious song.
And, O, God of Grace, it was fine to be
  In beauteous Ireland at that time!

OUR WEEKLY STORY.

THE SISTERS.

By Stephen Dedalus.

Three nights in succession I had found myself in Great Britain-street at that hour, as if by Providence. Three nights also I had raised my eyes to that lighted square of window and speculated. I seemed to understand that it would occur at night. But in spite of the Providence that had led my feet, and in spite of the reverent curiosity of my eyes, I had discovered nothing. Each night the square was lighted in the same way, faintly and evenly. It was not the light of candles, so far as I could see. Therefore, it had not yet occurred.

On the fourth night at that hour I was in another part of the city. It may have been the same Providence that led me there—a whimsical kind of Providence to take me at a disadvantage. As I went home I wondered was that square of window lighted as before, or did it reveal the ceremonious candles in whose light the Christian must take his last sleep. I was not surprised, then, when at supper I found myself a prophet. Old Cotter and my uncle were talking at the fire, smoking. Old Cotter is the old distiller who owns the batch of prize setters. He used to be very interesting when I knew him first, talking about "faints" and "worms." Now I find him tedious.

While I was eating my stirabout I heard him saying to my uncle:

"Without a doubt. Upper storey—(he tapped an unnecessary hand at his forehead)—gone."

"So they said. I never could see much of it. I thought he was sane enough."

"So he was, at times," said old Cotter.

I sniffed the "was" apprehensively, and gulped down some stirabout.

"Is he better, Uncle John?"

"He's dead."

"O . . . he's dead?"

"Died a few hours ago."

"Who told you?"

"Mr. Cotter here brought us the news. He was passing there."

"Yes, I just happened to be passing, and I noticed the window . . . you know."

"Do you think they will bring him to the chapel?" asked my aunt.

"Oh, no, ma'am. I wouldn't say so."

"Very unlikely," my uncle agreed.

So old Cotter had got the better of me for all my vigilance of three nights. It is often annoying the way people will blunder on what you have elaborately planned for. I was sure he would die at night.

The following morning after breakfast I went down to look at the little house in Great Britain-street. It was an unassuming shop registered under the vague name of "Drapery." The drapery was principally children's boots and umbrellas, and on ordinary days there used to be a notice hanging in the window, which said "Umbrellas recovered." There was no notice visible now, for the shop blinds were drawn down and a crape bouquet was tied to the knocker with white ribbons. Three women of the people and a telegram boy were reading the card pinned on the crape. I also went over and read:—"July 2nd, 189— The Rev. James Flynn (formerly of St. Ita's Church), aged 65 years. R.I.P."

Only sixty-five! He looked much older than that. I often saw him sitting at the fire in the close dark room behind the shop, nearly smothered in his great coat. He seemed to have almost stupefied himself with heat, and the gesture of his large trembling hand to his nostrils had grown automatic. My aunt, who is what they call good-hearted, never went into the shop without bringing him some High Toast, and he used to take the packet of snuff from her hands, gravely inclining his head for sign of thanks. He used to sit in that stuffy room for the greater part of the day from early morning, while Nannie (who is almost stone deaf) read out the newspaper to him. His other sister, Eliza, used to mind the shop. These two old women used to look after him, feed him, and clothe him. The clothing was not difficult, for his ancient, priestly clothes were quite green with age, and his dogskin slippers were everlasting. When he was tired of hearing the news he used to rattle his snuff-box on the arm of his chair to avoid shouting at her, and then he used to make believe to read his Prayer Book. Make believe, because, when Eliza brought him a cup of soup from the kitchen, she had always to waken him.

As I stood looking up at the crape and the card that bore his name I could not realise that he was dead. He seemed like one who could go on living for ever if he only wanted to; his life was so methodical and uneventful. I think he said more to me than to anyone else. He had an egoistic contempt for all women-folk, and suffered all their services to him in polite silence. Of course, neither of his sisters were very intelligent. Nannie, for instance, had been reading out the newspaper to him every day for years, and could read tolerably well, and yet she always spoke of it as the *Freeman's General*. Perhaps he found me more intelligent, and honoured me with words for that reason. Nothing, practically nothing, ever occurred to remind him of his former life (I mean friends or visitors), and still he could remember every detail of it in his own fashion. He had studied at the college in Rome, and he taught me to speak Latin in the Italian way. He often put me through the responses of the Mass, he smiling often and pushing huge pinches of snuff up each nostril alternately. When he smiled he used to uncover his big, discoloured teeth, and let his tongue lie on his lower lip. At first this habit of his used to make me feel uneasy. Then I grew used to it.

That evening my aunt visited the house of mourning and took me with her. It was an oppressive summer evening of faded gold. Nannie received us in the hall, and, as it was no use saying anything to her, my aunt shook hands with her for all. We followed the old woman upstairs and into the dead-room. The room, through the lace end of the blind, was suffused with dusky golden light, amid which the candles looked like pale, thin flames. He had been coffined. Nannie gave the lead, and we three knelt down at the foot of the bed. There was no sound in the room for some minutes except the sound of Nannie's mutterings—for she prays noisily. The fancy came to me that the old priest was smiling as he lay there in his coffin.

But, no. When we rose and went up to the head of the bed I saw that he was not smiling. There he lay solemn and copious in his brown habit, his large hands loosely retaining his rosary. His face was very grey and massive, with distended nostrils and circled with scanty white fur. There was a heavy odour in the room—the flowers.

We sat downstairs in the little room behind the shop, my aunt and I and the two sisters. Nannie sat in a corner and said nothing, but her lips moved from speaker to speaker with a painfully intelligent motion. I said nothing either, being too young, but my aunt spoke a good deal, for she is a bit of a gossip—harmless.

"Ah, well! he's gone!"

"To enjoy his eternal reward, Miss Flynn, I'm sure. He was a good and holy man."

"He was a good man, but, you see . . . he was a disappointed man. . . . You see, his life was, you might say, crossed."

"Ah, yes! I know what you mean,"

"Not that he was anyway mad, as you know yourself, but he was always a little queer. Even when we were all growing up together he was queer. One time he didn't speak hardly for a month. You know, he was that kind always."

"Perhaps he read too much, Miss Flynn?"

"O, he read a good deal, but not latterly. But it was his scrupulousness, I think, affected his mind. The duties of the priesthood were too much for him."

"Did he . . . peacefully?"

"O, quite peacefully, ma'am. You couldn't tell when the breath went out of him. He had a beautiful death, God be praised."

"And everything . . . ?"

"Father O'Rourke was in with him yesterday and gave him the Last Sacrament."

"He knew then?"

"Yes; he was quite resigned."

Nannie gave a sleepy nod and looked ashamed.

"Poor Nannie," said her sister, "she's worn out. All the work we had, getting in a woman, and laying him out; and then the coffin and arranging about the funeral. God knows we did all we could, as poor as we are. We wouldn't see him want anything at the last."

"Indeed you were both very kind to him while he lived."

"Ah, poor James; he was no great trouble to us. You wouldn't hear him in the house no more than now. Still I know he's gone and all that. . . . I won't be bringing him in his soup any more, nor Nannie reading him the paper, nor you, ma'am, bringing him his snuff. How he liked that snuff! Poor James!"

"O, yes, you'll miss him in a day or two more than you do now."

Silence invaded the room until memory reawakened it, Eliza speaking slowly—

"It was that chalice he broke. . . . Of course, it was all right. I mean it contained nothing. But still . . . They say it was the boy's fault. But poor James was so nervous, God be merciful to him."

"Yes, Miss Flynn, I heard that . . . about the chalice. . . He . . . his mind was a bit affected by that."

"He began to mope by himself, talking to no one, and wandering about. Often he couldn't be found. One night he was wanted, and they looked high up and low down and couldn't find him. Then the clerk suggested the chapel. So they opened the chapel (it was late at night), and brought in a light to look for him. . . And there, sure enough, he was, sitting in his confession-box in the dark, wide awake, and laughing like softly to himself. Then they knew something was wrong."

"God rest his soul!"

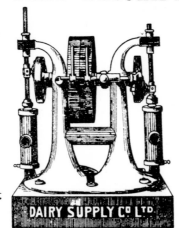

As Mr Bloom, early in the morning, turns from Eccles into Dorset Street, to buy his pork kidney, "the flabby gush of porter" floats up from Larry O'Rourke's cellar-grating, and Bloom reflects on the "general thirst" of his fellow-countrymen: "Good puzzle would be to cross Dublin without passing a pub." It would still be a good puzzle.

Dublin has always had a desperate thirst. In Charles II's reign, 1,180 ale houses and 91 public brew-houses catered for its 4,000 families, who also had the right to make their own whisky and beer. In Edward VII's reign, with a population of 300,000, it had 906 places selling liquor on the premises, and 366 with off-licences. Today, for a population of 700,000, there are 851 licensed houses, 221 with off-licences, and 136 clubs, a total of 1,208. Shane Leslie said Dublin's slum-

The Brazen Head, Dublin's oldest pub, was established in 1668. When they meet early in the morning after Bloomsday, "Lord John" Corley tells Stephen Dedalus and Bloom "you get a decent enough do in the Brazen Head . . . for a bob".

dwellers were born in "Original gin". Of its 5,174 citizens arrested for drunkenness in 1904, two-fifths were women, and a writer in *Talk* lamented that the curse of the drink habit among Dublin's womenfolk was assuming "alarming dimensions": "Silent, sly drinking in bygone days was bad enough, but the open and defiant exercise, which is now so common, of this habit in public places, is a blot upon our boasted civilization, and a standing reproach to our religious leaders and our law-makers."

The law-makers were urged to make it an indictable offence for a woman to enter a public house, and to "reward the publican caught supplying drink to woman with twelve months' hard labour".

A surprising number of Bloomtime pubs have survived, though face-lifts have destroyed the character of many. The most famous, Davy Byrne's, in Duke Street, where Joyce and Oliver Gogarty often spent Sunday mornings "having quiet ones", and where Mr Bloom had his sevenpenny lunch of "feety" green cheese and burgundy, is little changed in the upper stories, but the bar has become a glitteringly self-conscious rendezvous for the wide-eyed tourist, the bearded avant-garde and the dry-martini set, while the Bailey across the street, another Joycean haunt, where Parnell and his followers, and later Arthur Griffith and his, used to meet, has been completely rebuilt. The Ormond on Ormond Quay, where Joyce's father drowned his sorrows and dodged his bailiffs, and, bronze by gold, the elegant Miss Douce and Miss Kennedy presided, has also been sadly modernized—that is to say, emasculated. Even Larry O'Rourke's has a new front.

Mr Bloom would feel more at home today in Mulligan's of Poolbeg Street, where gas lamps still flicker on the old brown woodwork, though in unequal competition with chilly striplights, or in O'Meara's Irish House, at the corner of Winetavern Street and Essex Quay, with its façade depicting high moments of Irish history in gaudy relief. Not far from the Irish House, in a courtyard off Bridge Street, is the oldest and least changed of Dublin's pubs, the Brazen Head, where the down-and-out Corley tells Stephen Dedalus and Bloom in the cabman's shelter, you could get "a decent enough do" for a bob. The Brazen Head was old when Bloom was young. It was established in 1668. Robert Emmett is said to have drunk in its tiny parlour, where Oliver Bond, at a meeting of the United Irishmen in 1797, expounded his plan for taking possession of Dublin. In the same parlour, but in rather more vigorous idiom, Brendan Behan often gave expositions on life and literature, and took possession of a tiny bit of Dublin.

Two famous Bloomtime pubs have disappeared: Barney Kiernan's in Little Britain Street, the scene of Bloom's unhappy encounter with the Citizen and his dog, and the Ship Tavern, in Lower Abbey Street, where Buck Mulligan, after borrowing twopence for a pint, arranges to meet Stephen Dedalus at "half twelve". Barney Kiernan's, close to the markets, the Four Courts, and the Castle, had an unpredictably assorted clientele from all three establishments. The

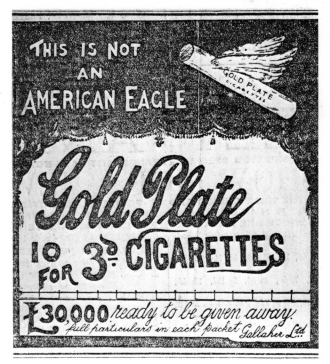

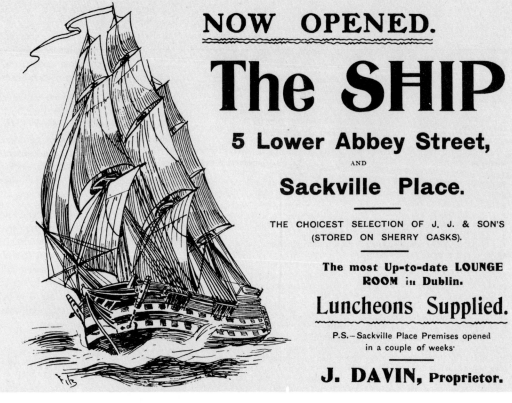

Ship, destroyed during the Troubles, had a long musical tradition. In 1831 it advertised that "the celebrated Irish harpist from Belfast" performed every evening from seven till 12 o'clock, and announced: "Soup sent on order to any part of the city of Dublin." In 1852 it offered visitors many amenities, "at the most moderate charges":

Hot joints from 12 to 5; dinner off the joints 1s.; hot lunch (roast and boiled) with vegetables 6d.; the Table d'hôte as usual from 5 to 7; Dinner (fish, soup and joints,) 1s. Breakfast, luncheons, Soups, Supper etc., equally moderate; Beds per night, 1s.

The Times, Bell's Life, Allison (Liverpool), Manchester Guardian, and a few copies of the *Daily Freeman* and *Saunders' News Letter* to be disposed of at half-price.

Persons desirous of a rich musical treat will have an opportunity of being highly gratified by dropping into the Coffee-room of the "Ship" any evening after seven, where Messrs EDWARD JONES AND THOMAS HIGHAM (two of the most accomplished Musicians of the day) will perform on their respective instruments—Harp, Dulcimer, and Higham's improved Accordian—an endless variety of the most popular Airs, Duets and Solos.

The Ship, formerly flanked by the editorial offices of *The Nation* on one side and the *Irish Times* on the other, was very popular with writers and journalists. "It is patronized by everyone—the prince, the patrician, the plebeian, and the politician", said the *Irish Daily Independent*. Among its less reputable patrons was the forger of the Parnell letters, Richard Piggot. Its premises went through to Sackville Street, a distance of about 200 feet.

The cost of eating, drinking, and sleeping had increased considerably by 1904. In Bloomtime, a bed at the Four Courts Hotel cost 2s. a night; table d'hôte luncheons were 1s. 6d., and table d'hôte dinners 2s. and 2s. 6d. At first-class hotels, such as the Shelbourne and the Gresham, bed and breakfast cost from 5s. 6d. to 6s. 6d. a night, and full board, 34s. a week.

John Jamieson's 8-year-old Whisky was 3s. 9d. a bottle, and Guinness, 1s. 10d. a dozen pints, or 2d. a pint from the wood.

POLICEMAN—"What's wrong with the motor; won't it go?"

TRAMP—"I don't know; but as I wos comin' away I think I heard them say all the POWER'S gone!"

The National Library and its twin building, the National Museum, flank Leinster House, the eighteenth-century residence of the Duke of Leinster, now the seat of the Irish Parliament.

" 'Tis passing strange that the splendid inducements offered to students by the National Library attract so few of our men to its book-lined precincts," lamented a writer in *St Stephens*, the student paper of University College, Dublin, in June 1904. "Here is to be found an atmosphere conducive to work, an atmosphere which converts drudgery into pleasure, indolence into energy." In Bloomtime, the library and its twin building, the National Museum, flanking the eighteenth-century residence of the Duke of Leinster, with the Leinster lawn between, were comparatively new. They were built in 1884. Today Leinster House, the most splendid of Dublin's mansions, accommodates the Irish Parliament, and a hideous concrete parking-lot for politicians' cars has replaced the lawn and flower-beds.

Joyce was certainly attracted to the library's book-lined precincts—as were Yeats, George Moore, Padraic Colum, Gogarty, and George Russell—and to the entrance porch with its "cream curves of stone", where the students met, talked, ate, and watched the birds, as they still do. In *A Portrait of the Artist*, as Stephen Dedalus stands on the library steps seeking an augury in the birds, their "dark frail quivering bodies wheeling and fluttering", the colonnade reminds him vaguely of an "ancient temple". Stephen's dogged exposition of Shakespeare, recorded in *Ulysses* ("He proves by algebra that Hamlet's grandson is Shakespeare's grandfather and that he himself is the ghost of his own father"), takes place in the room of the urbane—or obsequious—Quaker librarian, John Lyster, known as the Students' Friend. Lyster encouraged students to meet and talk, but imposed rigid silence in his round reading-room. If any reader spoke, Lyster

"Cream curves of stone."

"Shapely goddesses . . . curves the world admires."

would have a big SILENCE sign hung reproachfully over his desk.

During Stephen's scholarly discussion, Mr Bloom pays a hurried visit to the library to look up an advertisement in the *Kilkenny People*. He has just made a pilgrimage to the museum across the lawn to satisfy his curiosity on another scholarly question: How realistic were Greek sculptors in their representation of woman, viewed from behind? The circular entrance hall of the museum then displayed casts of classical statuary. "Shapely goddesses, Venus, Juno: curves the world admires," Bloom muses. "Can see them library museum standing in the round hall, naked goddesses. Aids to digestion. They don't care what man looks. . . . They have no. Never looked. I'll look today. Keeper won't see. Bend down let something fall see if she."

When the Venus which Mr Bloom discreetly investigates was given to the Museum in 1885 a writer in the *Dublin University Review*, in an ode of welcome, wrote:

> Some say 'tis shocking
> She has no frock on,
> Not e'en a stocking
>   Her beauty dims.

> They who reprove her
> Would wish to cover
>   (With dress-improver)
> Those shapely limbs.

> Still she'll refresh us
> Still smile propitious,
> Still look delicious,
> Conscious, yet coy.

> And in this dim age
> Of smoke and scrimmage,
> Our radiant Image
> Be Dublin's joy.

Venus is no longer Dublin's joy. She and her frockless companions were removed from the Museum in 1927; in their place now stand rather less joyful replicas of Celtic crosses.

Mr Bloom was not the only Dubliner who had an esoteric interest in Greek statuary. Lynch, in *A Portrait*, confesses that he once wrote his name in pencil on Venus's backside. Perhaps the naked goddesses were removed because of their vulnerability to such tributes.

"On the brewery float bumped dullthudding barrels rolled by grossbooted draymen. . . ." The dull thud of Guinness barrels made music in a city boasting the biggest brewery and one of the biggest thirsts in the world—as well as the world's first maternity hospital, though no Dubliner has attempted to correlate the three. The firm of Guinness was founded in 1759, in a small disused brewery at St James's Gate. Bloom, recalling that its head, Lord Iveagh, "once cashed a sevenfigure cheque for a million in the Bank of Ireland", makes some characteristic calculations: "A million pounds, wait a moment. Twopence a pint, fourpence a quart, eightpence a gallon of porter, no, one and fourpence a gallon of porter. . . . One and four into twenty: fifteen about. Yes, exactly. Fifteen millions of barrels of porter. What am I saying barrels? Gallons. About a million barrels all the same." Watching a barge with export stout pass under O'Connell Bridge, he thinks of getting a pass to see the brewery, "regular world in itself". Its output today is about two million barrels a year.

57285

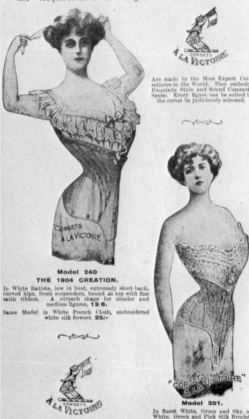

On Bloomsday, Mr Bloom was thinking of buying a violet silk petticoat for his wife Molly to match her new garters, and Molly was thinking of restraining her "opulent curves" in one of those "kidfitting corsets . . . advertised cheap in the *Gentlewoman* with elastic gores on the hips . . . they give a delightful figure line 11/6 obviating that unsightly broad appearance across the lower back. . . ." She decided also to knock off stout for dinner. Mrs Bloom obviously was not interested in the advertisement for "Ogilato" that appeared in *Talk*:

THE BUST

When well-developed is women's greatest adornment. It's so indicative, too, of good breeding, and other charming attributes that no lady lacking these traits can afford to be indifferent to this. To those thin of bust through sickness and other causation, Dr Brown's unique specific "Ogilato" will be a great boon. It will positively develop the bust from six to eight inches in one month; this we guarantee.

The price of corsets varied considerably. Weingarten's Erect Form corsets ("America's latest models—They are not only the most stylish of all corsets, but their hygienic construction places the strain on the muscles of the hips and back, where they are most capable of bearing it") ranged from 3s. 11d. to £7 7s. according to materials, among which were jeans, coutilles, batistes, and broches. Much engineering skill was employed in designing corsets that would resist the strains imposed on them. Thomson's "Graciosa" Corset (from 7s. 11d. a pair) had a Hip Section made in two parts, the lower one overlapping the other, "thus securing absolute Freedom from Breakage and perfect ease in any position of the body".

"The craze for white continues without abatement," said a writer in *Figaro and Irish Gentlewoman* in April 1904. "Smart rooms, particularly those of the upper ten, display nothing but white. . . . Anything like the introduction of crimson or strong yellow would prove gruesome." But coloured stockings were having a great vogue, and under the heading "A Dangerous Fashion" *Irish Society* warned its readers against them, especially bright red stockings, which had caused several cases of blood-poisoning: "The wearers of high-coloured hosiery always run a considerable risk as should the colour permeate the skin, through a scratch or cut, blood-poisoning is the probable result." Readers were advised to leave this mode severely alone, and to content themselves with fast-dyed black hose, sewn with scarlet—advice which Molly Bloom wisely heeded.

Two very charming creations for late spring or summer heat are here shown. The model with flowing pleats is quite seductive in its elegant simplicity, composed of pastel grey eolienne, defined at waist and belt of black velvet, and further finished by the pointed cape collar of white Irish crochet, this gown ranks amongst our smartest coming modes . . . the charming hat . . . is distinctly Frenchy and modish. A soft filmy lace depends around from a

felt crown, on which a soupçon of black is evident. . . . Medallions of shell pink chiffon are accentuated by light ornaments of filigree, silver and turquoises. A double narrow ruching of pink chiffon encircles the edge and is charmingly evident, the filmy lace toreador fall cunningly draped at the left side. The many charms of this delightful confection are further enhanced by the large rose of soft pink chiffon which nestles under the edge. The second gown is depicted in that daintiest of dainty fabrics, soft white mousseline de soie, with black spots. This is mounted throughout on champagne silk and further beautified by bands and belt of black ribbon velvet. The hat is detailed in finely pleated white chiffon. The brim swathed in black chiffon with

lace form a tasteful finish to the three quarter length sleeve, while the deep gaged flounce around the tail is a novelty in Empire effects. The tea gown is an evolution from the dressing gown; charming alike to the wearer and to beholder. To some extent it became supplanted by the ubiquitous coffee jacket. In favour of the latter its delights may possibly have waned. Now, however, they again burst forth with double favour in the gown which united Bohemia with Belgravia.

Figaro and Irish Gentlewoman, July 1904

dainty velvet knots beneath relieve the trying chastity of white. An ostrich tip of either black or white appears upon the otherwise flat crown. To complete the accompanying quartette a pretty tea gown is shown. Tea gowns, coffee jackets, in fact the *négligé* in every form is today quite a feature of the modern wardrobe. Very fascinating is this model, expressed in palest blue *crêpe de chine*. The cape-like collar may be carried out in oyster coloured satin, on which a trailing design in pale blue ribbon work is embroidered. A double frill in similar shade of accordeon-pleated chiffon renders the capelet decidedly *chic*. Wide frills of chiffon or

DAINTY THINGS FOR DAINTY DAMES.

e coloured shades will be much more seen this season than last. ery palest must, however, be used, and in many cases even these nts are veiled with white gauze or chiffon.

hings, frillings, puffings are more used than giving a soft, cloudy look to the dress which is effective and becoming. Frills are the most le form of trimming, as they can be pressed out tossed, which cannot be done in the case of puffs hes.

Artificial flowers are used in abundance, deep bands of them being placed at the head of flounces, or flounces bordered with a narrow edging of the smaller sorts. Bands are also worn reaching the whole length of the skirt from waist to hem.

Flowers perpendicularly placed, however, look much better when arranged in loose sprays with buds and foliage, and in these cases it is wiser to select plants

SMART CHAPEAU

own beaver, the crown surrounded a upright ribbon of bronze green, velvet to tone, finished with a

TAILOR-MADE HAT

of fawn felt, bearing smartly-tied velvet bows and two quills. These shapes are worn well over the eyes. But for smart occasions this winter felt will not be worn, Dame Fashion having decreed that the more airy type of chapeau and those built in velvet shall then be omnipotent. On most of the velvet chapeaux the beef-eater crown is seen, while the up-standing, pleated ruche of velvet figures on those of any and every persuasion.

pretty, but are less easily arranged than the sharp-pointed ones. A fichu is a useful addition to an evening dress, as the depth or height of the bodice can be arranged according to fancy.

Many evening bodices are made with a removable transparent neck-piece, so that a low body can be transformed into a high one at a moment's notice; a pair of transparent long sleeves are also a convenient means of changing a full into a *demi-toilette*.

Many sleeves for full-dress wear reach as far as the elbow, and are quite tight-fitting. Two or three very full frills finish them very prettily and becomingly. These frills can be of lace or of the same material as the dress itself.

Velvet is coming in for evening wear. It is, however.

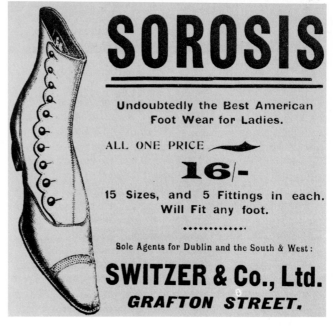

THE NEW TORPEDO TOQUE

of finest black silk beaver, trimmed with *coq de roche* miroir velvet in the form of a cocade and bow. A lovely black plume sweeps over the hair.

"The novel and very pretty blouse sketched on this page is of osier green taffetas, in the original model. The empiecement and stole ends of handsome cream-coloured guipure, edged with brown fur, are threaded with green soft ribbon, finished with loops and pom-pom fringe. The cape sleeves falling from the long, sloping shoulder-piece, are of the newest, as are also the wide under-sleeves, arranged with tucks forming deep cuffs and matching those in the front of the blouse. The deep folded belt is of soft silk."

37

A humorist once said that half the population of Dublin was clothed in the cast-off garments of the other half. This was substantially true. (Stephen Dedalus in *Ulysses* is wearing secondhand "breeks", and Buck Mulligan remarks, "God knows what poxy bowsy left them off.") Every day in Patrick Street all kinds of old clothes were offered for sale, with boots, food, furniture, and domestic utensils. "Some of the goods displayed one would hardly think worth picking up as a derelict," commented Sir Charles Cameron, Dublin's Health Officer. "Veritable rags are offered for sale." A journalist described the scene:

> Auctions were going on briskly, and as we passed one of our party got accidentally struck in the face by a flannelette blouse which had just been knocked down to a purchaser for the sum of one penny. We

were offered six boxes of matches for a halfpenny, and five squares of black lead for one penny, also slabs of fish of an unknown variety at 2d. a lb. and a corset for seven pence. Between the Cathedral gate and Bull Alley we could have purchased, in the open, prayerbooks, pig's cheeks, candlesticks, onions, crockery, and second-hand clothing of all varieties, apples, wallpaper, American bacon, bouquets of dried grass, pictures of Parnell and William O'Brien, cauliflowers, disabled pingpong rackets, iron bedsteads and old militia uniforms.

"Standish O'Grady had begun to write about the ignominy of the living conditions of the poor in Dublin," says Padraic Colum. "The poet 'A.E.' had been startled out of his vision by the spectacle presented. But as I went through Patrick Street the hopes and

prophecies were dead. Here were decaying houses, stinking yards back of them, where families were domiciled in single rooms, where casually employed men, spiritless women, sickly children made up households. . . ."

"The poverty of a large proportion of the population is shown by the large number of persons who are obliged to resort to the pawnbroker," Sir Charles Cameron wrote in 1904. "Some people pawn their clothes regularly every week":

No inconsiderable number of the poor get out of their beds, or substitutes for them, without knowing when they are to get their breakfast, for the simple reason that they have neither money nor credit. They must starve if they have got nothing which would be taken in pawn. But articles of very small value will be accepted by the pawnbroker, and some item or items of a slender wardrobe are exchanged for the price of one or more meals—so small a sum as sixpence may be obtained in this way. In general the sums advanced do not exceed 2s. When work is procured the articles are, as a general rule, released from pawn. The pawning of clothes and other articles is not peculiar to the very poor; it extends to many persons belonging to the artisans, and better classes. On Monday, or perhaps Tuesday, no money is left, and the best clothes are consigned to the pawnbroker. On the following Saturday, on the receipt of the weekly wages, the clothes are redeemed. Every Saturday night, the pawnbrokers' offices are crowded with persons, chiefly women, getting back the articles that had

39

been pawned earlier in the same week. Those who pawn their goods in hard times may never be able to redeem them. . . .

Sir Charles found that in a single year 2,866,084 pawntickets were issued in Dublin, representing loans totalling £547,453, or £2 4s. per head of population. Interest was fixed by law at fivepence per pound per month—25 per cent per annum. A month's interest could be charged even if the articles were redeemed within a few days.

Some pawnbrokers, such as Terence Kelly, in Fleet Street—"The Back of the Bank", and Belle McGuinness, "who walked like a queen"—were well-known Dublin characters:

Mrs McGuinness, stately, silverhaired, bowed to Father Conmee. . . .

And Father Conmee smiled and saluted. How did she do;

A fine carriage she had: Like Mary, Queen of Scots, something.

And to think she was a pawnbroker: Well, now!

In 1904 Sir Charles Cameron published a horrifying report on the housing of the poor. Nowhere in the world was the contrast between squalor and splendour more acute or the distribution of slums more widespread. "In most cities," he wrote, "the purlieus are in a limited number of districts, but in Dublin they are to be met with everywhere. The lanes at the rear of such fashionable squares and streets as Merrion Square, Fitzwilliam Square, Stephen's Green, Upper Mount Street . . . are now occupied to a large extent by the poorest classes." So were many of the former mansions. More than two-fifths of Dublin's 60,000 families—about 100,000 people—lived in single rooms, sometimes as many as ten or twelve people to a room.

The transition from mansion to tenement was the result of the Act of Union of 1800, which abolished the Irish Parliament and deprived Dublin of its 270 peers, its 300 members of the Commons, and their innumerable hangers-on. (It was estimated that each member of the Lords spent an average of £6,000 a year, and each member of the Commons £2,500.) Until then it had been an elegant, animated European capital—"the seventh city of Christendom", as Oliver Gogarty was fond of intoning—proud of its culture, its architecture, its hospitality, and its wit. After the Union, paralysis was followed by decay and Dublin declined rapidly to the level of a shabby provincial

43

town, the general depression caused by the Napoleonic war accelerating the process. "On the last stroke of midnight, December 31," writes Maurice Craig, Dublin's most eloquent biographer, "the gaily caparisoned horses turned into mice, the coaches into pumpkins, the silks and brocades into rags, and Ireland was once again the Cinderella among the nations."

The great ten- and twelve-roomed houses fell into the hands of "jobbers", who found it lucrative to let single rooms to labourers drifting from the provinces in search of work. By 1904 one-third of the population of Dublin consisted of unskilled labourers, hawkers, "hucksters", messengers, and other irregular workers, who lived—and died—in bitter poverty. Nearly half of all the deaths in Dublin each year took place in charitable institutions. The deathrate was 23.3 per thousand, compared with London's 16.1—and London, too, had its vast slum population.

The highest rate of wages for labourers was a pound a week. Many thousands of families had weekly incomes of less than fifteen shillings. Sir Charles Cameron quotes the budget of a married tailor who earned ten shillings a week. He paid 2s. 6d. a week rent, leaving 7s. 6d. for food, fuel, light, clothes, bedding, and everything else. Breakfast consisted of dry bread and tea, and the only other meal, dinner and supper combined, of dry bread, tea and herrings. Porridge was an occasional luxury.

MIRUS FETE,

In Aid of Mercer's Hospital,

At BALL'S BRIDGE.

NOW OPEN.

COME AND SEE THE

Beautiful Italian Scenery,

The Stalls from Nearly Every County in Ireland,

The Limerick Faction Fight,

The Spanish Bull Fight,

Children's Fancy Dances and Palace Ball Room,

Cafe Chantant, Cigar Divan,

Alhambra, Tea Gardens,

Refreshment Room,

Ice Cream Bower and Dining Hall,

Tableaux Vivants.

A Gorgeous Spectacle of Beauty and an Endless Round of Novel Shows and Amusements, including—

CLAY PIGEON SHOOTING, MOTOR DRIVES, GOLF PUTTING.

CROQUET TARGETS and BREAK COMPETITIONS.

DINNER in the DINING HALL

FIREWORKS ON WEDNESDAY EVG., 1st JUNE, and SATURDAY, JUNE 4th.

DOORS OPEN AT 2 O'CLOCK.
BAZAAR CLOSES, 10 30.

Admission ONE SHILLING.

William Humble, Earl of Dudley,
Lord Lieutenant of Ireland.

Just before he finished *Ulysses*, Joyce wrote from Paris to his obliging Aunt Josephine in Dublin, asking her to find out if it was possible for "an ordinary person to climb over the railings at Number 7 Eccles Street . . . lower himself from the lower part of the railings until his feet are within two feet of the ground, and drop unhurt". He wanted this information "to determine the wording" of a paragraph describing Bloom's homecoming on the morning after Bloomsday. How Aunt Josephine found out is not known, but she was able to satisfy Joyce that it was possible.

There are many such examples of Joyce's passion for accurate detail. A tree on Charleville Mall is described in the first printed version of *Ulysses* as an elm. Joyce later realized it should have been a poplar, and altered it accordingly. But despite this precision he was curiously indifferent to anachronism. William Humble, Earl of Dudley, Lord Lieutenant of Ireland, and his retinue drive through the pages of *Ulysses* in a glittering cavalcade to open the Mirus Bazaar at Ball's Bridge, and later in the day Cissy Caffrey and Gerty MacDowell, on Sandymount Strand, watch the

45

fireworks from the bazaar ("A monkey puzzle rocket burst, spluttering in darting crackles. . . . A long lost candle wandered up the sky from the Mirus bazaar in search of funds for Mercer's hospital. . . ."). But the bazaar had ended nine days before, and the Lord Lieutenant had been in County Clare all the week, behaving in a typically viceregal manner: playing golf, inspecting the houses of poor fishermen, expressing a polite interest in sewerage schemes, and bestowing half-holidays on bewildered schoolchildren.

"It is universally admitted that Mirus was quite the prettiest of the many big Bazaars yet held in the Royal Dublin Society's buildings," said the *Irish Society and Social Review* on 11th June. "Thousands of people patronized the Fête." But the behaviour of some evoked a stern comment from a columnist:

I know that in this matter I have the approval and support of many who were shocked and shamed on the closing nights of the Fête. . . . Abuse of the bars at Tea Stalls is a disgraceful blot upon the fairness and symmetry of philanthropic undertakings, and things were bad and unseemly indeed on last Friday evening at "Mirus" when at one stall alone three principals and upwards of forty assistants refused to take up duty on Saturday if a bar were not entirely removed. . . . Some persons—alas many!—are found to think anything and everything justifiable as long as it brings in money, but whether a more refined section is entitled to protection or not, or is to be pitied or otherwise for being exposed to rudeness and affront from semi-drunken men, whose condition has been conduced to, and their score of maudlin folly run up at bars attached to Tea Rooms, is a question which I leave all right-minded persons to answer.

The Viceregal Lodge, now the President's House, in Phoenix Park. It was built in 1751, and enlarged in 1816.

The Viceroy's gold-and-white throne room in Dublin Castle, once the symbol of English rule in Ireland. Dublin Castle is a collection of buildings, some dating back to Anglo-Norman times.

47

Davy Stephens at his news-stand.

Dublin has always bred "characters" and cherished, or at least tolerated them—from "Buck" Whaley in the eighteenth century to Brendan Behan in the twentieth. The city is small enough to give eccentricity a stage, and genial enough to smile at it. Bloomtime produced a singularly rich litter. Among those who move through the pages of *Ulysses* are "Professor" Denis J. Maginni, Cashel Boyle O'Connor Fitzmaurice Tisdell Farrell, and "Sir" Davy Stephens.

Maginni was a dark, mincing, elegantly apparelled dancing master who acquired an Italian panache by dropping the final "s" from his Irish surname: "Mr Denis J. Maginni, Professor dancing, etc., in silk hat, slate frockcoat with silk facings, white kerchief tie, tight lavender trousers, canary gloves and pointed patent boots, walking with grave deportment most respectfully." Joyce omits the spats and silver-mounted silk umbrella that completed the ensemble.

Farrell, known as "Endymion", was, sartorially, even more striking. Sometimes he wore a tailcoat over white cricket trousers, sometimes a lace jabot, knee breeches, and buckled shoes. Like Sir Winston Churchill, he was fond of hats. On Trafalgar Day he wore a cocked hat; on lesser occasions a deerstalker, a great bowler with big holes for ventilation, or a cricket cap. He usually carried a fishing-rod, two swords, and an umbrella. According to legend, he was a wealthy brewer's son from Dundalk, who had fallen into a family vat and never been quite the same after.

In his autobiography, *Head or Harp*, Lionel Fleming recalls a typical Endymion frolic:

On one occasion he bought, and paid for, a small joint of meat, requesting the butcher to set it aside to be called for later. Half an hour afterwards, a patrolling policeman observed Endymion rushing into the shop, spearing a joint of meat with his sword, and carrying it off down the street with yells of triumph. On being pursued and caught, Endymion produced the receipt. Then, as always, the crazy logic of his actions seemed to assert that authority was not only there to be defied, but was an absurdity in itself.

For nearly half a century Davy Stephens had a news-stand at Kingstown, with an informal charter to operate on the mail steamers. In *A Biographical Sketch*, said to be written by himself, he modestly claimed to have supplied newspapers and periodicals to "monarchs, princes, potentates, viceroys, all grades of the aristocracy, Lord Chancellors, Prime Ministers, Commanders-in-Chief, Cardinals, Archbishops . . . artists, authors, jockeys, prizefighters, aeronauts, tight and slack rope-walkers, and dancers . . . and 'long'

and 'short drop' hangmen." (The order of precedence is interesting. Authors creep in just before jockeys, but well ahead of hangmen.) As well as selling papers, he used to hire out the more expensive journals for a nominal rent.

Davy, who had a nimble wit and few inhibitions, enjoyed great licence. As he said himself, he was "equally at home when addressing the Emperor of Brazil [who offered him the post of Court Jester] or Count von Bismarck [who paid him with French coppers]". He claimed to have interviewed, "inter alia", Lord Palmerston, Lord Beaconsfield, Lord John Russell, Lord Tennyson, Cardinal Manning, Lord Wolseley, Sir Robert Peel, Longfellow, and Miss Ellen Terry. He had a warm and apparently reciprocated regard for Edward VII, both as Prince of Wales and as King, but was less enthusiastic about the Duke of Edinburgh, who once pressed into his hand a coin which Davy expected to be half a sovereign but which proved to be a threepenny piece. Lord Northcliffe, when he visited Ireland for the Gordon-Bennett Cup, invited Davy to accompany him in his car, and when someone occupied Davy's stand during one of his

Davy greets King Edward VII.

49

"*Himself*", *an unidentified citizen of Edwardian Dublin.*

under his cape, "a king's courier", and in the phantasmagoria of the "Circe" scene he cries: "*Messenger of the Sacred Heart*, and *Evening Telegraph* with St Patrick's Day supplement. Containing the new addresses of all the cuckolds in Dublin."

The Regency spirit survived in "Bird" Flanagan, a son of a respectable Dublin alderman, but a practical joker in the grand manner. He rode a horse through the swing-doors of the Gresham hotel and stole a small dark child from a Zulu village in a Dublin Exhibition, delivering it to the French pavilion in protest at France's declining birthrate. Oliver Gogarty records the incident that gained Flanagan the nickname of "Bird": "He went to a fancy dress ball at the Earlsfort Terrace skating rink dressed as the Holy Ghost and supported by two of the Holy Women. In the middle of the floor he laid an egg about the size of a football. The management interposed; he and his supporters were expelled. He went out clucking."

Lesser Dublin eccentrics were the barrister William Travers Humphreys Lyttleton Cox, who assiduously photographed Dublin's once-vigorous lavatory *graffiti*, and Michael Cusack, founder of the Gaelic Athletic Association, who made a practice of crashing his heavy blackthorn on a bar counter and shouting to the startled curate: "I'm Citizen Cusack from the Barony of Byrne in the County of Clare, you Protestant dog!"

The Dublin of Bloomtime had little trade or industry.

"*Endymion*".

regular attendances at the English Derby, Michael Davitt raised the matter in the House of Commons. Davy's activities were reported regularly in the *Irish Society and Social Review*. A paragraph in the issue of 31st October 1903 reads: "Davy had a great shake hands from Mr John Morley the other day. Davy congratulated him on the life of Mr Gladstone, and presented him with a copy of his own life, just published. Mr Morley said he would read it carefully, and perhaps he might see a review of it in one of the greatest of London's dailies."

Davy makes two appearances in *Ulysses*. From the office of the *Freeman's Journal*, in the "Aeolus" episode, he emerges, "minute in a large capecoat, a small felt hat crowning his ringlets", with a roll of papers

"One quality which would have struck the visitor to Edwardian Dublin was the air of indolence about the place," says Ulick O'Connor in his biography of Gogarty:

There were no factory chimneys to blacken the landscape. The atmosphere was leisurely. . . . There was an almost Latin disregard for time. . . . The presence of the university and the garrison contributed to the leisurely mood; the gowned student sauntering out for a talk and coffee into the centre of the city, the colourful cavalry strolling through the streets with jingling spurs . . . suggested a life that was not tied to a routine of the counting-house. . . .

One of the hazards of Dublin life in those days remains today. Cattle are still driven through its busy streets ("lowing, slouching by on padded hoofs, whisking their tails slowly on their clotted bony croups"). Mr Bloom offered constructive comment:

—I can't make out why the corporation doesn't run a tramline from the parkgate to the quays, Mr Bloom said. All those animals could be taken in trucks down to the boats.

—Instead of blocking up the thoroughfare, Martin Cunningham said. Quite right. They ought to.

A contemporary writer in *Irish Society* was more emphatic in denouncing this "egregious system":

What security have you, or have I, that when we leave our homes in the morning we may not be in hospital before noon, in a gored and bleeding condition? The existing condition of things is simply shocking. Little children in perambulators may be killed at any moment, and no practical notice is ever taken of the evil. "Mad Bull"?! "Mad Cow"?! is the cry, but infinitely madder are some of the people who utter it. . . . These creatures are not mad at all: they are goaded to temporary frenzy by terror and ill-treatment. They are taken off the grass to which they are accustomed, and transported from quiet, noiseless, country fields to harsh roadways, slippery pavements, stony thoroughfares, and the lurid turmoil of a city—with the added terror of men and boys shouting angrily behind them, and beating them cruelly with sticks. Can you, or can I, buy a bit of meat in any victualler's shop, even the best class, that is not defaced with purple stains, and congested bloodmarks and bruises? No, we cannot, and if you have to pass under the railway-bridge at Adelaide Road on a Wednesday evening, when terrified cattle are being driven from the railway premises to the market, you will view sights that will melt your heart to compassion, even if it be made of stone. . . . There ought to be a strict law against the present system of driving cattle through the thoroughfares and of committing them to irresponsible drovers, whose one idea is to hurry them to their destination by beating them unmercifully with rough sticks. . . .

"Curious the life of drifting cabbies, all weathers, all places, time or setdown, no will of their own," Mr Bloom reflects as he passes the cabman's shelter in Brunswick Street.

The sharp-tongued Dublin cabbies were as much a part of the Dublin scene as the sharp-tongued Dublin biddies crying their wares in Moore Street. The poet Austin Clarke remembered them on wet days, wrapped in heavy overcoats or oilskins, and on winter evenings, when "the brass and silver lamps, with the tallows in long sockets, threw a faint glow". As a boy, Sir William Orpen was driven home from the station every night at about ten o'clock, by when, he says "every decent driver was fairly well 'laden' ". He recalls one idiosyncratic driver in particular:

The cabman's shelter in Sackville—now O'Connell—Street. In a similar shelter near Butt Bridge ("an unpretentious wooden structure") Mr Bloom and Stephen Dedalus, after leaving Bella Cohen's brothel, are served with "a boiling swimming cup of choice concoction labelled coffee . . . and a rather antediluvian specimen of a bun", and talk at length about life.

. . . the lad who drove me was "weighed down with the weight of drink" but the old horse knew me all right and brought me safely home. When I jumped off and started to look for money to pay, the lad lashed me across the back with his whip, and continued doing this till I got out of range. Between my sobs of pain I asked him what he meant by these acts of violence. He leant over from his seat, beamed at me with love and friendship, and said, "Master Willie, Master Willie, sure you're so nice I must bate you!" He would have said much more only the horse was anxious to get to bed and moved off.

Dublin was still a city of horses, though the number of cabs had decreased from 766 in 1903 to 656 in 1904, and the number of outside—or jaunting—cars, from

A jaunting-car, Dublin's equivalent of the London hansom cab, outside the National Library.

There were 656 cabs in Dublin in 1904. By about ten o'clock at night, Sir William Orpen recalled, "every decent driver was fairly well laden"—with alcohol.

1,361 to 1,030. Drivers were strictly disciplined. In 1904, 1,194 were prosecuted for offences which included "improperly feeding beast", "Driving to Public Danger", "Not filling Hazard by prescribed Route", "Not having steps and Footboards turned up while disengaged", and "Interior of Vehicle Dirty". Cabs and cars had the same scale of fares:

By Distance (or Setdown)
For a drive for one or more persons, not returning with Hirer, for every statute mile going, 6d.
Drivers may charge 1s. for first mile or fraction of a mile going, when hiring shall terminate between 10 p.m. and 9 a.m. or at any hour when there are more than two persons.
Driver to bring back Hirer for a fare of 3d. per mile returning at any hour.

By Time
For the first 10 mins. or under, for not more than two adults . . . 0s. 6d. Between the hours of 10 p.m. and 9 a.m. to be increased to . . . 1s. 0d.

"Astonishing the things people leave behind them in trains and cloakrooms," muses Mr Bloom. He might have added cabs, too. In 1904, 175 umbrellas and sticks, five opera-glasses, two gold bracelets, one gold ring, and many coats and rugs were left behind in Dublin cabs, and five half-sovereigns were received by (honest) drivers in mistake for silver coins.

A four-in-hand is about to set out from the Shelbourne Hotel for Bray, on the Wicklow coast. Dubliners still coached for pleasure; the craze, which had begun in the late seventies, died with the Edwardian age. "For these sporting occasions," writes Elizabeth Bowen in her admirable history of the Shelbourne, "Ladies went tailor-made":

coaching indeed, created its own fashions, exiling fussy, draped skirts, frail bonnets, or flighty hats. Sheltered indoor complexions, so pink-and-white, were recklessly cast to the havoc of the wind and sun—parasols were discarded, veils blown to shreds.

Trim buttoned boots were displayed as one mounted the coach; silhouettes flared out into 'postilion basques', and mannish waistcoats of plush were worn.

Dublin gentlemen prided themselves on their proficiency in "handling the ribbons". Sir Thomas Talbot Power, a very wealthy man with a love of horses, drove his coach-and-four from the Shelbourne to Bray and back, charging 10s. 6d. a seat. This included dinner at the International Hotel, Bray, with champagne. It was in the Shelbourne that Mr Bloom bought Mrs Miriam Dandrade's old wraps and underclothes.

Demon tricyclists scorch through Phoenix Park.

"The cycle," said Arthur James Balfour in June 1904, "is the most civilizing invention of the age." By this standard, Dublin was a very civilized city. Cycling was in its heyday. When "Skin-the-Goat" was released from prison in 1902 he was asked what surprised him most about Dublin. His reply was "the small bicycles" that nearly everyone was riding, and the electric trams. When he went to prison the only cyclists in Dublin were a few intrepid athletes perched precariously on their high "penny-farthings".

Now the safety bicycle, ridden by women as well as men, swarmed in every street, and cycle-stealing had become a profitable profession. In its issue of 15th June 1904 the *Irish Cyclist*, commenting on a sentence of "five years durance vile" imposed on a Mr Ferns, an enterprising thief who had developed a technique of selling his stolen machines to policemen ("when arrested almost a hundred bicycles could be traced to his nimble fingers"), said:

In no city in the kingdom is there so much careless-ness displayed with the storing of cycles as in Dublin. Every office hall is full of good machines, and it invariably strikes the visitor to Dublin as a strange sight to see so many unattended bicycles outside the door of nearly every Dublin restaurant between the hours of one and two. The owners of these machines are inside lunching, without a thought to the safety of their trusty steeds.

You could buy a "trusty steed" for as little as £6 6s., but a reliable model cost from £15 15s. to £22 10s. A tandem, or tricycle, cost at least £20. Most were imported from England, a fact that the *Guide to Dublin* for 1904 deplored:

Everyone is aware of the enormous importance of the bicycle in modern life; but perhaps we do not all know that the bicycle, in its modern form, may be said to have had its origin in Dublin, and that Dublin missed by a very little being made the chief seat of an industry that has since grown to vast pro-portions in another land. At the time of the inven-tion of the pneumatic tyre, Dublin was still under the old delusion that all trade was "low"; the aesthetic sense of some of the citizens was shocked by the idea of a factory in the heart of the city, and the Dunlop Pneumatic Tyre Co. was actually forced to transfer their works to an English Town. Perhaps there is no article, in connection with which the old prejudice against the Irish-made goods is more striking, than the bicycle. We have firms like the Shamrock Bicycle Co. or Messrs Waytes or Keating, turning out bicycles as good in every respect and as cheap as those of the best foreign make; no one disputes the fact and yet three out of every four of the cyclists you meet will be riding a mount with an English name.

Oliver Gogarty was an ardent and skilled cyclist, and the College races were one of Dublin's most important social events, attended by the Viceroy and his court. Society women launched the new summer fashions at the two-day meeting, and bookies vigor-ously laid the odds at the back of the crowds.

Motor-cycles were still a novelty. "Hardly three and a half years have passed since the earliest crude-looking machines were first offered to the public," said the *Irish Cyclist* in June 1904. "The early machines were considered more or less playthings. . . . A non-stop ten miles run was a phenomenon."

The tricar, with its prettily decorated front seat, was a sociable compromise between motor-cycle and car.

The motor age was chugging in. Early in 1900 the first issue of *Irish Motor News* had appeared with a prophetic poem:

> *Gather ye knowledge while ye may*
> *Old-fashioned sports are lying dying*
> *And those who drive their motors today*
> *Tomorrow may be trying flying.*

The president of the British Association, in a series of bold predictions three years later, agreed; the motor-car would be ubiquitous by 1953 and obsolete by 2003, when "the problem of aerial navigation having been solved, all extra-luxurious transit will be at altitudes of from 3,500 to 5,500 feet". In 1953 the steam-engine would be non-existent, the bogs of Ireland exhausted, and its population have reached 8,000,000. Meanwhile, as the *Irish Cyclist* noted in

September 1904, "the rhythmic clang of the hoof" was being merged in "the whirring hum of fast-moving wheels". In October two Oldsmobiles on a 3,000-mile demonstration tour of the British Isles drove from Belfast to Cork, by way of Dublin, averaging a hundred miles a day. But cars were still objects of curiosity to most Dubliners. Joy rides in motor-cars were one of the attractions of the Mirus Bazaar in 1904; Sir Horace

Plunkett led a team of motorists who raised £146 18s. by taking 3,000 passengers for a drive of a mile and a half.

"The arrival of a new 8 h.p. Swift motor-car for a member of our staff created quite a commotion in Abbey Street the other day," *Irish Motor News* reported, in a paragraph headed "Shadow of a Crime":

Amongst those who stopped to have a look at the

These two Oldsmobiles in October 1904 drove from Belfast to Cork, by way of Dublin, averaging a hundred miles a day.

car was a well-known Dublin detective. After taking a glance at the engine, he called us aside, and whispered in our ear: "You have got a distinguished spectator admiring your car." "Whom do you mean?" we asked. "Do you see that man with the careworn face—well, that is Skin-the-Goat, the jarvey who drove the Phoenix Park murderers." After this conversation we took more interest in his face than we did in the brand-new car. The twenty years' imprisonment had left cruel marks on his furrowed countenance. . . . As he closely inspected the little car, strange thoughts passed through our minds. We wondered what his thoughts were, and if he was contemplating how different his fate might have been on that eventful May evening in 1882 could he have trusted his escape to a fast motor instead of a horse and cart.

(Skin-the-Goat, whose name was James Fitzpatrick, appears in *Ulysses* as the proprietor of the cabman's shelter, near Butt Bridge, where Mr Bloom and Stephen Dedalus go for coffee after their first climactic meeting in Nighttown.)

When Dublin motorists were prosecuted for driving in St Stephen's Green at eight miles an hour the Irish Automobile Association made a check on horse-drawn traffic and announced triumphantly that it often exceeded nine miles an hour, milk carts being the worst offenders. "To a nervous old lady," commented the *Irish Times*, "the appearance and noise of a car going at even eight miles an hour are probably not much less alarming than if it were going at eighteen. In a few years time, when the motor is as common . . . as the bicycle is now . . . we will think as little, perhaps, of twenty miles an hour as we do now of four." But it counselled drivers against excessive speed: "You may traverse Dublin in almost any direction in twenty minutes, even at six miles per hour. It is hardly worth while to travel at twice that rate, to frighten pedestrians, and perhaps incur a prosecution and a fine, for the sake of, say, ten minutes."

A Lady Cyclist complained that many motorists seemed to take a delight in seeing how closely they could "shave past" her machine, and *Figaro and Irish Gentlewoman* recalled that when bicycles became common they produced a type of rider known as a "cad on castors"; a reckless speed-mad hairbrain who "brought the pastime of cycling into disrepute, and made the average man a natural enemy of every wheeler". Now the motorist had produced a new type of "demon on wheels", the "scorcher", who "shows off by madly driving through the street to discover how often he may graze a human being without actually knocking him down". The most dangerous "scorcher" was the one who "alters the number on his machine so that if he does damage he may escape and the rightful owner of the identification number used

60

DUNHILLS MOTORITIES

EVERYTHING BUT THE MOTOR

Any Article gladly sent on approval

Country orders promptly executed by experienced assistants.

Drencher-proof Motoring Coat.

Perfect protection against any weather.

283 Full length, double-breasted, extension collar and wind cuffs, lined camel hair fleece £5 5 0

284 Full length, double-breasted, interlined with leather, making it doubly proof against driving rain £8 8 0

The Panhard Drencher-proof Coat.

244 Very smartly made in fawn, or grey drencher-proof tweed, lined camel hair. An ideal motoring coat.

Price £7 17 6

Tweed cap, as illustration 0 12 6

Motorist's Hand Protector.

677.

Fastened to steering wheel. Protects hands and wrists of driver, without interfering with steering.

677 Waterproof Leather Cloth, lined fur .. £1 15 0

696 Leather, lined fur £2 10 0

The Decauville Model Mackintosh.

Extremely practical combination Coat and Hood, made in light Mackintosh materials, gives complete protection from heavy rains.

393 Light fawn rubber proofed material, .. £3 13 6

394 Heavy Mackintosh, a variety of patterns, £5 5 0

ALFRED DUNHILL, Ltd.,

Automobilists' Tailors and Outfitters,

393. Hood down.

Head Depot & Wholesale Dept. :
359-361 Euston Road, London, N.W.
Telephone : 527 King's Cross,

Telegrams : "Dunsend, London."

Numbers Two and Five, Conduit Street, Regent Street, W.
Telephones : 3859 and 3381 Gerrard.

393. Hood up.

AGENTS :—CROTTY & CO., GRAFTON STREET, DUBLIN.

61

The first licensed lady drivers in Ireland.

by him may get into trouble". There had been several recent instances of this.

Registration of cars was less than a year old. When it was introduced at the end of 1903, *Talk* offered a useful "Hint to Motorists":

Already there seems to be a wide desire to secure places in the first hundreds at least. A moment's thought ought to suggest to these people that a small number is more likely to be remembered than a large one, particularly if the owner is anything of a scorcher. The police have sharp eyes, and the detection of a motorist whose machine is No. 2 . . . would be a much easier matter than if the number were 28697. In the case of accidents, then I would recommend a long number in preference to a short one.

A few days after Bloomsday a columnist in the *Irish Motor News* reported on another useful hint:

My suggestion about motorists carrying whips has already been put into practice by the Rev. E. F.

Eilson-Hill, who writes me as follows:— "I now carry a long whip and I find that I easily keep off the road all animals, even dogs and cows, without being obliged to stop the car. The mere sight of the whip in your hand will make most animals keep close to the hedge. That has been my experience, and I now drive with far greater comfort and with little or no danger to animals. It felt like a game of polo at first, with my left hand on the steering wheel and a long stick in my right hand."

Mr Hill, who drove a 12 h.p., two-cylinder Gladiator costing £395, found the motor-car invaluable for pastoral work, and a doctor who drove a Decauville Sociable with a fringed canopy extolled it for medical men: "A doctor's horses are usually so done up at the end of a week that a drive for pleasure cannot be thought of," he wrote. "Moreover a car can be pulled up infinitely quicker than a horse."

There were reckless horse-drivers, too. The *Irish Times* reported that Patrick Horan, $7\frac{1}{2}$, had his head fractured when he was run down by a trap driven by Mr Patrick Odlum's cook and housemaid: "It appeared that the girls turned back in the trap to carry on a flirtation with a Protestant clergyman's coachman, who had driven past them, and the boy was knocked down and run over."

Motorists were demanding greater comfort. As *Ireland Illustrated* pointed out: "In the early days of motoring no one cared particularly about cold and wet: If a car kept going, the occupants were so thankful that they paid no attention to minor inconveniences." But as engines grew more reliable they also became more powerful, "and as cars travelled faster, motorists began to feel the wind whistle through them, and then the era of leather clothes, frieze overcoats and goggles commenced". However, really heavy clothing—"huge overcoats, rubber-necked ponchos, and the like"—were not popular, especially with doctors, who had to study appearance, and with the ladies, who "absolutely refused to adopt such forms of motor clothing". The closed brougham body offered complete protection from cold and rain, but it was "rather unsuitable for anything except town work", and *Ireland Illustrated* suggested a compromise: "Even the ordinary hood affords wonderful protection. It breaks the wind and the motorists sitting in its shelter, so to speak, carry their own air along with them. . . . In the same way, too, it affords considerable protection from rain, although its merits in this respect are much enhanced if used in combination with a glass screen. . . ." Hoods, of course, offered a great deal of wind resistance, and should be in position "only when urgently needed".

Weather, police, dogs, and cows were not the only hazards that bedevilled the motorist of 1904. There was also the Chauffeur Problem, a new and specialized subdivision of the eternal Servant Problem. "Motor manufacturers are almost daily improving their cars," said *Ireland Illustrated*, "but unfortunately no one has yet evolved a method of producing an improved pattern of chauffeur." A disinclination to put up with the "expense and annoyance" of having a professional chauffeur attached to the household prevented many people from buying cars:

It is not difficult to appreciate the point of view of the man who would like a car, but not a chauffeur, and therefore has neither. To begin with, a chauffeur is an expensive article—most of them demanding thirty shillings to two pounds a week, with their board and lodgings, as wages. Secondly, he has got an evil reputation for an anxiety to increase his wages by trading on his master's ignorance of motor matters. This can easily be done by ordering more petrol in a month than the car would use in a year, buying spare parts which are not wanted, and tyres which are never used. Unfortunately, some motor dealers aid and abet chauffeurs in this outrageous swindling, and the motor owner who is so doubly unfortunate as to have a chauffeur who is a thief, and a motor dealer who is devoid of principle, finds the pastime very expensive. Possibly, the greatest objection of all to the professional chauffeur is that, although in the position of a servant in many instances, he knows neither his place nor his manners. In as much as he has probably been brought up at the bench, or served in a garage, this certainly is not to be wondered at, but the fact remains, that between the manner and bearing of the chauffeur and the well-trained coachman or groom there exists a gulf so wide that most people cannot tolerate it. Independence and self-respect are fine things in the abstract, but as interpreted by the ordinary chauffeur, they are altogether intolerable.

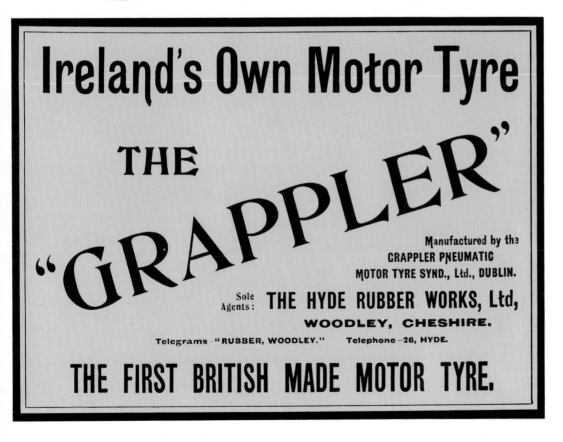
63

Chauffeurs may have been hard to find, but there was a wide range of cars—some steam-driven—and of body-styles, from the 6 h.p., single-cylinder Vulcan at £110 to the 17 h.p., three-cylinder National at £550. Makes included Wolseley, Daimler, Lanchester, Vauxhall, Darracq, Martin, Star, Panhard and Levassor, Siddeley, Cotterau, Duryea, and Ariel. Wolseley made a Phaeton, a Waggonette, a Tonneau, a Shooting Brake, a Coupe, and a Landaulet. The most popular American car was the Oldsmobile, a tiller-steered "petrol-buggy", at £150. The resolute motorist was always photographed "on" not "in" his machine, a distinction not without significance.

"This useful type of Parcels Delivery Van is used by the enterprising proprietor of Prescott's Dye Works, and was supplied by Messrs Callow & Sons, Dublin. The Chassis, is a standard 8 h.p. Darracq, with a single cylinder motor, and fitted for 3 speeds and a reverse. The vehicle has now been in use for some two months, and covers about 60 miles per day on a consumption of about 2 gallons of spirit. It has proved very satisfactory; and according to the report of the driver has so far required no adjustment or repair," said the *Motor News* on 17th October 1904.

Prescott's enterprising Dye Works enjoyed Molly Bloom's custom. Leopold recalls that when he sent his daughter Millie to Prescott's, "for Molly's Paisley shawl", Millie ("clever little minx!") brought home the change in her stocking.

The Pavilion at Kingstown (now called by its original name, Dun Laoghaire) was an ornate pleasure-dome and concert-hall. Subsequently it showed moving pictures and was replaced by the present cinema, still called the Pavilion. Just before Bloomsday Joyce hoped to get a singing engagement at the Pavilion (see page 2).

This elegant drinking-fountain was erected outside the Pavilion to celebrate Queen Victoria's third visit to Ireland in 1900. Her great-uncle, George IV, the first English monarch to land in Ireland with goodwill, landed speechlessly drunk, and suffering, in Mr Maurice Craig's words, "from distressing looseness". Mr Craig relates that when His Majesty went to Curragh "a sanitary engine was prepared for his comfort, Lord Mayo observing that 'the usual dimensions would suffice, as His Majesty, though corpulent, was finely turned.' But Lord Meath knew better, and Mr Massey Dawson . . . who 'declared his willingness to contribute by any means in his power' was measured for the purpose."

"Mr Bloom stood at the corner, his eyes wandering over the multicoloured hoardings." As an advertising canvasser Bloom often brooded over "the infinite possibilities hitherto unexploited of the modern art of advertisement". Many of his own ingenious ideas had been rejected, such as the suggestion of an illuminated transparent showcart with two smart girls sitting inside writing letters to advertise Hely's the stationers, or an ink bottle with a false stain of black celluloid. He would have agreed with an article in the *Leader* which said, "As a nation we are hopelessly backward in the importance of advertising, and know little of the art." The *Leader* commended the imagination of a poetic publican named McGrath, who had composed this lyric:

My Ales and my Brandies
My Wines and my Rums,
Are the finest with which,
Men could moisten their gums.

Few Dublin copy-writers matched Mr McGrath's inventiveness. The most notable were those who composed the advertisements for patent medicines. It was a Golden Age of quackery and gullibility, and the claims of the nostrum makers were magnificently uninhibited. A popular technique was to disguise an advertisement as a news item, such as this paragraph in *Talk*:

DEATH AND THE CAMERA

Of all the many purposes to which the camera is applied, that of providing a picture of features of loved ones, to be preserved after they have been re-

"What is home without Plumtree's Potted Meat? Incomplete. With it an abode of bliss," *Mr Bloom "read idly".*

moved by death, is amongst the most useful. In this connection an interesting experience has been related by a Hull woman. She was considered so ill her death was a mere question of time. In view of the fact, her friends persuaded her to have her photograph taken. She did so, but soon after, she began to try Chas. Forde's Bile Beans and in consequence she is today as healthy as ever in her life.

Another advertisement for Mr Forde's Bile Beans, in *Ireland Illustrated*, was headed "Australia's Greatest Discovery", and read:

Australia, the Land of Gold, has given to the world a great number of marvellous things, but the discovery made in that wonderful country by a Chemist and Scientist, Mr Charles Forde, perhaps will do more good to the world generally than all the Gold Australia ever has or ever will produce. "Bile Beans" have been proved an undoubted cure for Headache, Biliousness, Costiveness, Piles, Liver Troubles, Bad Breath, Rheumatism, Influenza, Indigestion, Dizziness, Buzzing in the Head, Fulness after Eating, Lack of Ambition, Debility, Female Ailments, Pimples, and a host of other Ailments that owe their origin to Defective Bile Flow, Assimilation and Digestion. They will also be of great service in Nervous Disorders, Loss of Appetite, Debility, Shortness of Breath, Blotches on the skin, Insomnia, and Troubled Sleep. They act quickly in restoring Females to Health, and for a General Aperient and Tonic Remedy they are almost unequalled.

Many specifics were available for "restoring Females to Health". That fair specimen of winsome Irish girlhood, Miss Gerty MacDowell, found that Iron Jelloids "had done her a world of good much better than the Widow Welch's female pills".

Dublin has always loved funerals — and wakes. "Whether it is that more people die in Dublin than in other cities, or simply that they die more expensively and with more pomp, I have no idea," said an anonymous Englishman in a book of *Dublin Explorations and Reflections*. "But I have never before in my life been in a town where hearses and coffins and mourning coaches were so much in evidence."

All day, and particularly on Saturdays and Sundays, he noted the long processions winding up Sackville Street on their way to Glasnevin; they were "generally recognized as a Dublin speciality".

Seamus O'Sullivan wrote whimsically:

As I go down Glasnevin Way
The funerals pass me day by day,
Stately, sombre, stepping slow,
The white-plumed funeral horses go.
With coaches crawling in their wake,
A long and slow black glittering snake
(Inside of every crawling yoke
Silent cronies sit and smoke)
Ever more as I grow thinner
Day by day without a dinner
Every day as I go down
I meet the funerals leaving town;
Soon my procession will be on view.
A hearse, and maybe a coach or two.

68

A contributor to the *Evening Herald*, Joseph O'Connor ("Heblon"), described a funeral he passed in Dorset Street: "'Twas a rambling, disorderly, festive funeral—a little child, possibly well insured. Children supported by capacious mothers leant out of the cab windows, jocular conversation went on between the occupants of one outside car and another, old women gossiped and laughed, and the jarveys smoked their pipes with every appearance of satisfaction." Though, according to Stanislaus, James Joyce disliked funerals, the "Hades" episode in *Ulysses*, which describes Paddy Dignam's funeral, is one of his finest pieces of writing.

"Mr Bloom walked unheeded along his grove by saddened angels, crosses, broken pillars, family vaults, stone hopes praying with upcast eyes, old Ireland's hearts and hands." With other mourners, he had earlier stood by Parnell's grave:

With awe Mr Power's blank voice spoke:

— Some say he is not in that grave at all. That the coffin was filled with stones. That one day he will come again.

Hynes shook his head.

— Parnell will never come again, he said. He's there, all that was mortal of him. Peace to his ashes.

When Mr Bloom looked at the grave of the Chief, it was marked by a cross. This has been replaced by a great boulder of Wicklow granite, with PARNELL cut in big capitals.

"The quays were crowded with cars, and coming up out of the traffic was an organ-man between the shafts, a young Italian woman tugging with one arm at the strap, a red handkerchief on her head, her hair blown back from her temples, her broad passionate face thrown upwards with the effort of pulling, tired, thoughtless, happy," Stanislaus Joyce noted in his diary.

Barrel organs, sometimes accompanied by a performing monkey in red military coat, blue-braided trousers and a pillbox hat, dispensed their music in many Dublin streets. As Paddy Dignam's funeral turns from Blessington Street into Berkeley Street, "a street-organ near the Basin sent over and after them a rollicking rattling song of the halls. Has anybody here seen Kelly? Kay ee double ell wy . . ." An anonymous Italian organ-grinder is among the twenty-four Dublin citizens listed as temporary occupants of Molly Bloom's bed.

The itinerant musician was not always appreciated. A writer in the Dublin weekly, *Talk*, blamed the "noise" of the barrel organ for much of the fashionable complaint of "neurasthenia", which, "like appendicitis", was "absolutely indispensable to a reputation for up-to-dateness". Neurasthenia, also known as "nerves" or "brain fag", had driven people to rubber heels and hypophosphites "and made the fortune of many a patent-medicine vendor". The barrel organ was an unmitigated evil from every point of view:

It provides a dishonest living for a class of people, composed chiefly of bogus peers and undesirable aliens; it is a source of annoyance to everyone who has ears to hear, and it perpetrates unspeakable outrages on our most cherished musical composers. It respects neither sickness nor death, and its powers of endurance are infinite. . . .

George Moore was one of its most distinguished victims. When he quarrelled with his neighbours in Ely Place, the three Misses Beans, because he insisted on painting his door green instead of the accepted white, he used to rattle his stick along their railings late at night to make their dogs bark. The ladies counter-attacked brilliantly by hiring organ-grinders to play under his windows when he was polishing his marmoreal paragraphs. The outraged Moore prosecuted the organ-grinders.

Many other sounds made up the strident orchestration of Dublin. Horses, their hoof-irons "steelyringing", drew hackney cabs, outside cars, lorries, delivery vans, milk carts, hearses, and a wide variety of private vehicles. Under the heading "Carriages for Sale", Mr Robert Grant, 38 Dawson Street, advertised landaus, broughams, polocarts, victorias, waggonettes, parisians, and double dogcarts. Street vendors loudly proclaimed their wares; fish-hawkers pushing old perambulators and crying, "Dublin Bay Her-r-in" and "Fresh Cock-cock-cockles"; black-shawled women balancing baskets on their heads, crying, "Ye-oung wather grass! Ye-oung wather grass!" (an archaic form of "watercress"); young girls at the foot of Nelson's Pillar crying, "Ripe plums, ten for a panny." On O'Connell Bridge an old woman stood from early morning till midnight, crying, "Buy a box of matches from this poor blind woman." Rabbits and kids nailed to a board, those inner organs that Mr Bloom ate with relish exposed to view, were hawked through the streets, followed by escorts of flies. There were boot-lace-sellers, flower-sellers, holly-and-ivy-sellers, and beggars innumerable. "Can anything be done," asked a writer in *Irish Society*, "to save peaceable householders and unoffending pedestrians from the many forms of beggary that are abroad?":

It is impossible to pause for an instant to exchange a word with a friend in the street without a third party at once taking part in the conversation! You don't in the least know whether he comes up from the sewer grating, or evolves himself out of the flags, but there he is at your elbow, telling you all his family concerns, including the baby's ailments, and the postponed interment of his wife's aunt, which has not yet taken place, owing to want of funds.

If you set out to drive, every pause is made a

70

"Ripe plums, ten for a panny", at the foot of Nelson's Pillar. It was here that the "two Dublin vestals", Anne Kearns and Florence MacCabe, used to buy their four-and-twenty plums to take off the thirst of their one-and-fourpenceworth of brawn.

misery by reason of bunches of lavender and groups of baskets thrust in at the window of your vehicle, and if you walk, and the day is wet and windy, and you are struggling over a muddy crossing or along a storm-swept street, you will as sure as fate be pursued by somebody who expects you to drop skirt and umbrella and parcels, and grope out money for his particular benefit. This kind of mendicancy is peculiar to Ireland. Other places are exempt from it, and to say that the poverty of the country is accountable is an ancient fallacy that sensible persons have long ago ceased to quote. Nothing will ever stamp it out, I fancy, because the first step towards the accomplishing of so desirable an end would mean the revolutionizing of a nation—the making of Ireland self-reliant and self-respecting. We are a charming people—comely, warm-hearted, kindly, affectionate, and anecdotal!—but our cry when we want anything is "Can't you do it for me?" and in the matter of self-respect we are as backward as a country child at school. From the well-to-do lady, who borrows your necklace or your frying-pan with equal *sangfroid*, and makes capital out of her friends—to the well-paid servant who is persistently untidy and attends the door in broken boots, you can trace the want of self-respect which among all ranks is so deplorable.

The deficiencies of the "well-paid" servant were a constant theme in the correspondence columns of Dublin papers. A writer in *Irish Society* attempted a judicial summing-up:

I think we have to thank ourselves for the gradual obliteration of all ancient domestic landmarks. . . . We never cease to shriek about "Higher Education", "Equality", and "Independence" in the case of upper-class women, without seemingly considering the certainty of the influence of our teaching filtering down to an humbler stratum. . . . We ourselves have obliterated the days of serfdom and miserable wages and general domestic drudgery, ill paid, ill clad, and ill conditioned. Red-handed Molly, down at heel, dirtily clothed and perspiring from grimy toil, exists no longer among the gentry —our maids must be well dressed, must wear spotless cuffs and collars, and be neatly shod. We may be country folk, so poor that we cannot keep a horse to carry us, and so happy-go-easy that the ducks are squatting around the stove in the hall, and the donkey wandering in at the back door to run his chance of a stray potato, but if Martha Jane brings in tea with any point about her to be criticized, why, we tell it to her later. . . .

I am very largely with servants on the question of standing up for their reasonable rights, and requiring proper remuneration for well-rendered services, but I am not at all with them in their wonted forgetfulness of certain facts; notably that in these days of desultory training, they learn their business at their employers' expense, practise on materials provided at other people's cost, damage and break with absolute impunity (employers replacing everything they injure), get regular holidays while members of families do the work, and are fed and paid, however short may be the finances for other purposes. These are things that ought not to be lost sight of— although they usually are.

Employers, on the other hand, forget the natural claims of servants for suitable and timely recreation, or healthful sleeping-apartments, and for occasional snatches of undisturbed and quiet relaxation. It may not be possible to define such periods . . . but it is quite within the limits of possibility in ordinary households to refrain from unnecessary bell-ringing and unessential "chivvying" at some hour of the day which the servant can soon come to count upon, more or less, as her own, although always at the ready service of her employers. . . . I may just add, in answer to K.L., that I consider it a downright cruelty to lock away papers, etc., from servants who would enjoy looking over them at the close of the day's work. We clamour persistently for educational benefits for the serving classes, and yet grudge to the servants of our own house the recreational privilege of a few minutes' quiet reading. . . .

Either of these girls could have been
Edy Boardman "with the baby in the
pushcar" who prattles so prettily "A jink a
jink a jawbo" when he wants a drink
of water.

73

When Mr Bloom passes the office of the *Irish Times* in Westmoreland Street he reflects: "Best paper by long chalk for a small ad." The *Irish Times*, Ireland's first penny paper, founded in 1859, is still the best paper for small ads—and for big news, and informed comment. But the two papers that Mr Bloom read, the *Freeman's Journal* and the *Evening Telegraph*, have ceased to exist, together with their contemporaries the *Daily Express*, the *Morning Mail*, and the *Dublin Evening Mail*.

The *Freeman's Journal* and the *Evening Telegraph*, established in 1763, were published from the same big, rambling office, extending from Prince's Street to Middle Abbey Street; the scene of the "Aeolus" episode in *Ulysses*. Bloom, who canvassed advertisements for both papers, finds a copy of the four-page *Evening Telegraph*, "Last Pink" edition with late sporting results, in the cabman's shelter. Among the headlines he glances at are "Great battle Tokio. Love-making in Irish £200 damages. Gordon Bennett. Emigration swindle. ... New York disaster, thousand lives lost", and an account of the Ascot Gold Cup won by the outsider Throwaway, at twenty-to-one.

Headlines in file copies of the "Last Pink" *Telegraph* for Bloomsday are curiously at variance with some of these: The Russo-Japanese war story, on page two, is subheaded "Big battle at Telissa"; the breach-of-promise story, on page three, is headed "Gaelic League and Love Affairs"; and the excursion-steamer story, on page four, "Appalling American Disaster".

The disaster was the burning in New York's East River of the pleasure steamer *General Slocum*, crowded with women and children on a Sunday-school excursion. The *Evening Telegraph*, in a leading article headed "The American Horror", commented on it eloquently:

It is just as well for us that we cannot adequately appreciate in all their horror such big disasters as occur in America, and the latest of which, reported last evening, must have sent a thrill around the world. As usual on such occasions, some difficulty is experienced in ascertaining the exact number of the victims of the disaster on the East River, one estimate putting it at 500, whilst the latest sent last evening places the death roll at 1,000. But it was as surely a holocaust as that overwhelming calamity in the Iroquois Theatre in Chicago in the winter holiday season. We are accustomed in these counties to prepare ourselves for a certain number of fatalities —inevitable under the circumstances—during holiday time, but none of the magnitude and overpowering horror of that which befell the New York

Westmoreland Street. The ball on the roof of the last building on the left was a time-ball. "Now that I come to think of it," Bloom muses, "that ball falls at Greenwich time. It's clock is worked by an electric wire from Dunsink."

75

SPECIAL EDITION.

The Freeman's Journal

AND

NATIONAL PRESS.

2

VOL CXXXVII.   DUBLIN: THURSDAY, JUNE 16, 1904.   ONE PEN

excursionists who gaily set out yesterday morning on a trip up the East River to a pleasure resort on Long Island. American "bigness" is in it—the characteristic with which the American is so familiar in many things that when he comes to other countries and beholds smaller proportions and slower movements he pronounces them "one-horse," "slow," thus winning for himself the character of a boaster if not worse, though in reality he is indulging in a very natural criticism.

Old Europe willingly concedes America's greatness in accidents by fire and flood, the natural result of doing things on a great scale. On the pleasure steamer that went up the East River yesterday morning with flags flying and hundreds of children singing and cheering for very joy there must have been at least one thousand souls. The steamer was apparently one of the kind so familiar on American rivers, broad-beamed and many-decked, and her passengers, the greater number women and children, formed the annual Sunday School excursion party of the St Mark's German Lutheran Church. It was near Hell Gate that the catastrophe came. The unlovely name of this portion of the river has been given a real dread significance. The rocks hemmed in the burning steamer—she could not turn—and what followed was a veritable hell of suffering and horror. How did it happen? The cause ascribed is as likely as any other—some fat boiled over in the lunch room, made a blaze, and according to the pastor of St Mark's Church, in three minutes all the decks were flaming. In the narrow passage of the river the wind must have become a fierce draught, which gave the flames their terrible hold on the steamer. So the captain's plan when he steamed full speed away from Hell Gate rocks and beached his

steamer at North Brothers' island could only be partially successful. . . .

But the story that Mr Bloom would have digested with most relish was the report of the action for £500 damages taken by Miss Maggie Delaney, of Abbeyville, Co. Kilkenny, against Mr Frank P. Burke, a

MISS MAGGIE DELANEY
(PLAINTIFF)

revenue officer, also of Kilkenny. Though appearing on page three, it was really the "lead" of the paper, occupying nearly three columns, including two specially drawn illustrations.

Miss Delaney, who was under twenty-one, was described by her counsel, Mr T. C. Moloney, K.C., as a person of many beauties and charms, with a nice contralto voice; Mr Burke as a Gaelic enthusiast who had devoted his spare moments to the spread of the Irish language. A few of Mr Burke's spare moments were also devoted to Miss Delaney, whom he encouraged to take singing lessons. Her voice, according to a poetic examiner, was like a piece of Kilkenny black marble, "capable of much polish". While it was being polished, Mr Burke presented Miss Delaney with music books and gloves, wrote her twenty-five amorous letters, partly in Gaelic, kissed her, and finally, in October 1902, suggested marriage. Miss Delaney said she knew nothing about house-keeping, but accepted him. Two years later she found he was walking out with another girl, whom he subsequently married. "Laudable as the Gaelic movement was," the eloquent Mr Moloney told the jury, "and laudable as its desire was to preserve the Irish tongue, it was not to be made a tent under which men like the defendant were to be allowed to outrage the best feelings of men, and to tear and break women's hearts." The jury awarded the torn and broken-hearted Miss Delaney £200 damages.

Molly Bloom might have been interested in the report that "a well-known Dublin lady", Mrs Daniel Bolger, had applied for membership of the Dublin Stock Exchange. The *Evening Telegraph*, offering her "all encouragement and a hearty welcome", said:

There ought to be no difficulty about her admission. Women are in many cases specially qualified for business dealings. They have often an instinct for a bargain and a caution in securing good value that the mere man can only envy. There are not many firms in this country or in England which are run by women, but it is commonplace enough in France and in America to see a woman at the head of a large commercial concern.

But Mrs Bolger was a disappointed avatar. Her application, after being displayed on the wall for the usual ten days, was rejected.

And Stephen Dedalus, who that day delivered his memorable discourse on *Hamlet*, would surely have read the review in the *Freeman's Journal* of the per-

**MR. BURKE, THE DEFENDANT,
Conducting His Own Defence.**

LAST PINK.

EVENING TELEGRAPH.

EW SERIES—NO. 7131.   DUBLIN: THURSDAY, JUNE 16, 1904.   2   ONE HALFPENNY.

THE WAR.

PORT ARTHUR AGAIN OPEN

RUSSIAN CRUISER ENGAGES THE JAPS.

SEVERE FIGHTING NEAR KAICHAU.

ENGAGEMENT IN THE KOREAN STRAITS.

TWO JAP TRANSPORTS MISSING.

(PRESS ASSOCIATION WAR SPECIAL)

Tokio, Wednesday.

The entrance to Port Arthur is open. The Russian cruiser Novik emerged yesterday and engaged the blockading Japanese ships.

ADMIRAL TOGO'S REPORT.

engaged the Vladivostock squadron off Tsushima. This report is so far unconfirmed. The transports, Ugomaru and Fuyomaru, homeward bound, met the Russian fleet this morning near Iki Island. The Russian squadron pursued and fired sixteen shots at them, but they escaped to Katsumoto.

1,000 JAP PRISONERS FOR KIEFF.

(PRESS ASSOCIATION WAR SPECIAL)

St. Petersburg, Wednesday.

A thousand Jap prisoners, including some twenty officers, are shortly expected to arrive at Kieff. Other prisoners who will be brought to the same district later will be cantonned at Kharkoff, Poltava and Kursk. The first army corps of St. Petersburg, which consists of two divisions of infantry, two brigades of artillery, and one brigade of cavalry, will be sent to the front. It will remain under the orders of its present commander, General Baron Meyendorff, who though entitled on account of his age to be relieved from taking part in the present campaign, persisted in going to the front, in order, it is said, that he might earn on the battlefield the Cross of the Military Order of St. George, which is the only decoration that he does not possess.

SEVERE FIGHTING.

APPALLING AMERICAN DISASTER.

EXCURSION STEAMER ON FIRE.

500 LIVES LOST.

WILD SCENES OF PANIC

CHILDREN THROWN OVERBOARD.

WOMEN TRAMPLED TO DEATH.

(PRESS ASSOCIATION FOREIGN SPECIAL)

New York, June 15.

Five hundred persons, mostly children, perished to-day by the burning of the steamer General Slocum, near Hell Gate, on the East River. The disaster is the most appalling

The Motor Car Race

EXCITING SCENE IN HOMBURG

Racing Cars in Danger from Blazing Petrol.

(REUTER'S TELEGRAM.)

Homburg, Thursday.

The whole morning to-day was occupied with the weighing of the racing machines which will take part in the Gordon-Bennett Race. This was carried out at the town weighing machine in the narrow Elizabeth Strasse, and began with a most alarming incident.

Mr. Edge was waiting with his Napier car,

GAELIC LEAGUE AND LOVE AFFAIRS.

Breach of Promise Action from Kilkenny.

AMUSING CORRESPONDENCE.

Verdict for £200.

To-day Mr. Justice Wright and a city common jury heard the case of Delany v. Burke. The plaintiff, Miss Margaret Delany, who is not yet 21, sued through her father, a cabinetmaker, at Abbeyview, Co. Kilkenny, the de-

---

formance in the Gaiety Theatre the night before. The critic observed that Mrs Bandmann-Palmer had chosen the part of the Prince of Denmark for herself, and "to say the least, sustained it creditably". But:

> With respect to the ghost, one is tempted to wish that modern scientific resource could step in and substitute some kind of illuminated optical spectre for the flesh and blood figure that stalks the stage in a white dress and boots. True, the ghost has to make a speech . . . but that could be done by someone behind the scenes, and it would sound in a muffled way that would suit the situation exactly.

The advertisement columns of both papers are instructive. You could get a passage from Dublin to New York for £2 (inclusive), buy an old Cremona violin ("*Nicolas Amati Fecit*, 1640") for £1 17s. 6d., a ton of the Best Wigan coal for 19s., a bath chair for 30s., a bespoke suit for 35s., an inside car for £8, and a glass hearse "at a low price".

Kelly Brothers, of Upper O'Connell Street, subscribing to the genteel pretence of the period that you drank wine for health, not for enjoyment, advertised

WINES FOR INVALIDS

	Per Doz.
VINO DE PASTO SHERRY, 1886	36s.
EAST INDIA GOLDEN-*do*-1883	36s.
INVALID PORT, TAWNY	36s.
OLD MADIERA, 1895	42s.
VIRGIN MARSALA, 1890	20s.
CHATEAU PONET CANET CLARET	30s.
CHATEAU MOUTON ROTHSCHILD	36s.
BURGUNDY MACON, 1898	24s.
BURGUNDY BEAUNE, 1892	30s.

Under the heading "Domestic Servants Wanted", advertisers offered 3s. 6d. a week for a General Servant ("Must be clean and tidy and sleep at home") and £5 a year for a "Respectable Country Girl to assist nurse with children and help with housework".

Under the heading "Situations Wanted", Experienced Generals, able to cook, wash and milk, offered their services for £12 a year; a Grocer's Assistant with five years' "city experience at both counters and cellar", sought a vacancy at £20 a year, and a Respectable Young Man offered "£5 Reward" to anyone getting him a job as van driver "at about £1 a week". For a fee of £15, two-year indoor apprenticeships were offered in dressmaking, grocery, and confectionery. Indoor apprentices were kept, but not paid.

Dentists and "medical" men advertised their skills persuasively. The Anglo-American Dental Company (most Dublin dentists claimed American associations) offered "Sets from 10s. 6d. upwards; Single Tooth, 2s.; painless extractions by gas, 5s.; with cocaine, 1s. 6d.; Scaling, 2s. 6d.; filling decayed teeth, 2s. 6d." All work was warranted for ten years, country patients were allowed part of their railway fare, and there were reduced fees for "people of limited means". Mr Henry J. Bradlaw, Surgeon Dentist Ltd, wished to notify patients that "extractions of stumps are unnecessary, a fact interesting to nervous subjects". Mr Bradlaw also published a testimonial from Alice Harding, of Clamore Castle, Ashford, Co. Wicklow:

> Dear Sir—I am pleased to say that my teeth are perfect for eating and speaking. I have got quite strong since I got them. My friends greatly admire them, and say they would hardly know they were artificial, they are so perfect in every way.

Dentist Macdonnell published testimonials from the Rev. Dr Sidley, Rector of Granard, and the Rev. Thomas Tynan P.P., Newbridge, both of whom thanked him publicly for his skilful, kindly, and inexpensive work.

Opposite the Shelbourne Hotel, proudly flying the Stars and Stripes, were the premises of the American Electro-Vibration Institute, whose modest advertisement, disguised as a news item, read:

THE AMERICAN DOCTORS AND THEIR GOOD WORK
Visit them soon if you want a free trial

The American Doctors will soon have been in Dublin two years. No institution for the healing of the sick in Ireland can point to a record as great as theirs. There are literally hundreds of people in Dublin and elsewhere in Ireland who are to-day happy men and women cured of chronic diseases that they believed to be incurable until they attended the Institute at 15 Kildare Street. Electro-Vibration is certainly a blessing to humanity. Dublin Physicians who have investigated, recognize that the American Doctors are accomplishing wonders, from the fact that their electric equipment is as near perfection as it is possible to attain, and everything new in Electrical Science that can better the physical condition of humanity is in constant use. The Methods of Electrical Equipment are their own inventions, and patented in all civilized lands.

WONDERS ARE DAILY PERFORMED

In curing all forms of Rheumatism and Neuralgia, in making Paralytics walk, in curing Consumption, Bronchitis, and Asthma, as well as Indigestion, Dyspepsia, Catarrh, and Ulceration of the Stomach and Constipation. If you are Debilitated, Run Down and Bloodless, Electro-Vibration will make you strong and vigorous again. This is certain.

Stanislaus Joyce writes that his brother James had a supreme contempt for violence and war. The picture at left, published in the Evening Telegraph *about the time of Bloomsday, was headed "The Terrors of Modern Warfare". It depicts a Russian bombing raid during the Russo-Japanese War.*

80

Mr Bloom "crossed at Nassau street corner and stood before the window of Yeates and Son, pricing the field glasses . . . Goerz lenses, six guineas. Germans making their way everywhere. Sell on easy terms to capture trade." It was in Nassau Street, on 10th June 1904, that Joyce spoke to a tall young auburn-haired girl from Galway who worked at Finn's Hotel. Her name was Nora Barnacle. When Joyce left Ireland four months later, she went with him. They were married 20 years later.

Sipping his burgundy in Burton's restaurant in South Anne
Street (the Waggon Wheel occupies the site today),
Mr Bloom recalls a romantic interlude with Molly. "Hidden
under wild ferns on Howth. Below us bay sleeping sky. . . .
She lay still. A goat. No-one. High on Ben Howth
rhododendrons a nannygoat walking surefooted,
dropping currants."

Babscaden Bay, Howth.

NOTE.—This Tender is to be delivered at the District Head Quarter Office,

by **12 O'CLOCK NOON** on _____ the _____ day of _____ 18

addressed to the "*General Officer Commanding*," and marked on the outside "*Tender*

for House at _____"

(**Any omission in this respect may lead to the offer not being duly considered.**)

TENDER FOR ~~HOUSES.~~ *Renting No 11 Martello Tower Sandycove.*

To ~~His~~ *His* Majesty's *Principal Secretary of State for the War Department.*

SIR,

I, *Oliver Gogarty*

of *5 Rutland Square E. Dublin*

am willing to become the Tenant of and occupy the Messuage mentioned in the Schedule to this Agreement, from the *Twenty fourth* day of *June 1904*

~~next~~ for one whole year, and so on from year to year, determinable as hereinafter mentioned, upon the terms and conditions following, that is to say :—

1st I will pay the clear yearly rent of *Eight pounds (£8)* by four equal quarterly payments, on the twenty-fifth day of December, the twenty-fifth day of March, the twenty-fourth day of June, and the twenty-ninth day of September in each year; and if the tenancy shall determine during any quarter, then also a proportionate part of the said rent up to the day of such determination; the first payment of rent to be ~~made~~ on the *Twenty ninth* day of *September* next. *for such portion of the quarter as may be due from the date of my receiving possession of the premises.*

2nd I will pay all quit rents, taxes, duties, levies, assessments, impositions, and outgoings whatever, now or at any time hereafter charged, levied or assessed on the said premises, or on or payable by the Landlord or Tenant in respect thereof (save only Landlord's income tax and tithe rentcharge).

3rd I will not assign, underlet or part with the possession of the said premises, or any part thereof, without leave in writing under the hand of the said Secretary of State, his successors or assigns (hereinafter designated the Landlord) first had and obtained for that purpose.

4th I will not commit or suffer any wilful or voluntary waste to be committed, on the said premises or any part thereof, and I will well and sufficiently repair, maintain, cleanse, amend, and keep the said premises, with the appurtenances, in good and substantial repair, together with all fittings, fixtures, and things, when and as often as need shall be; and in every third year paint all such parts of the outside; and in every seven years paint all such parts of the inside of the said premises as are usually painted, with two good coats of oil colour, and paper such parts thereof as require paper, and colour such parts as require colour, in a workmanlike manner.

5th I will at all times during the tenancy, keep insured the premises from loss or damage by fire, in an office to be approved of by the Landlord, in my name and his name jointly, in the sum of *One hundred (£100)* pounds, and produce the policy and the receipts for the annual premium from time to time; and in case of accident by fire I will rebuild the said premises under the direction and to the satisfaction of the Landlord in accordance in all respects with plans, drawings, and specifications previously submitted by me to him, and approved and signed by him or on his behalf.

Forms
K. 2405

This is the agreement between "His Majesty's Principal Secretary of State for the War Department" and Oliver Gogarty, signed on 24th June 1904, by which Gogarty became the tenant of "No. 11 Martello Tower, Sandycove", at a yearly rent of eight pounds. Joyce moved in on 9th September.

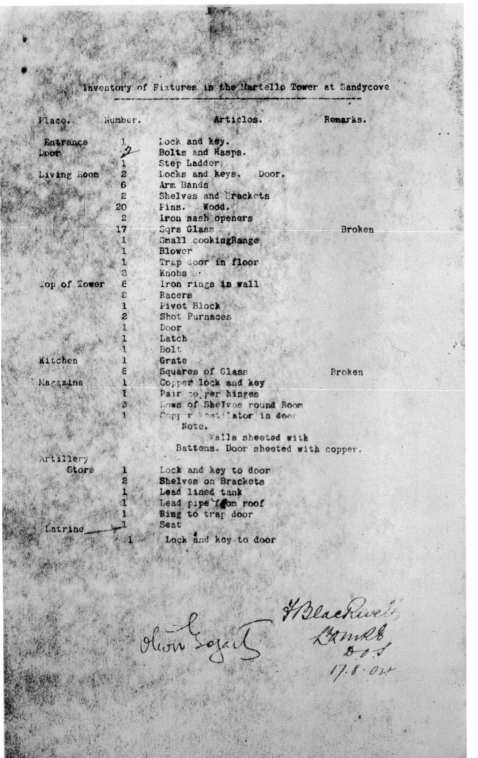

```
        Inventory of Fixtures in the Martello Tower at Sandycove
        ─────────────────────────────────────────────────────────

Place.        Number.            Articles.            Remarks.

Entrance       1         Lock and key.
Door           2         Bolts and Hasps.
               1         Step Ladder
Living Room    2         Locks and keys.    Door.
               6         Arm Bands
               2         Shelves and Brackets
              20         Pins.    Wood.
               2         Iron sash openers
              17         Sqrs Glass                    Broken
               1         Small cookingRange
               1         Blower
               1         Trap door in floor
               2         Knobs
Top of Tower   8         Iron rings in wall
               2         Racers
               1         Pivot Block
               2         Shot Furnaces
               1         Door
               1         Latch
               1         Bolt
Kitchen        1         Grate
               8         Squares of Glass              Broken
Magazine       1         Copper lock and key
               1         Pair copper hinges
               3         Rows of Shelves round Room
               1         Copper Ventilator in door
                            Note.
                         Walls sheeted with
                    Battens. Door sheeted with copper.
Artillery
    Store       1         Lock and key to door
                2         Shelves on Brackets
                1         Lead lined tank
                1         Lead pipe from roof
                1         Ring to trap door
Latrine         1         Seat
                1         Lock and key to door
```

The inventory of fixtures in the tower includes a "copper lock and key". The enormous key was made of copper so that it would not give off sparks and ignite the gunpowder once stored there. In the first chapter of Ulysses *Buck Mulligan asks Stephen for the key "to keep my chemise flat".*

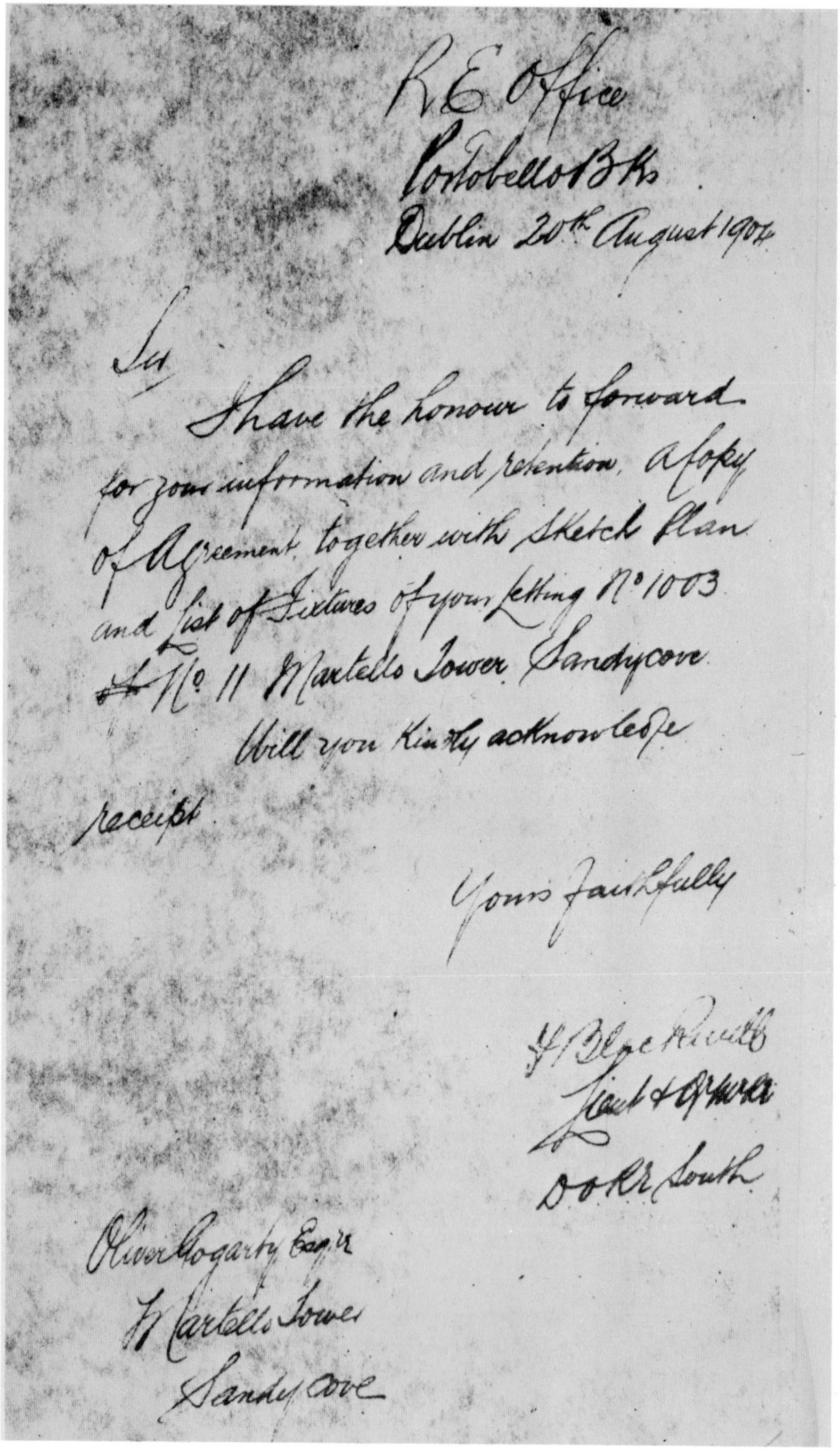

R.E. Office
Portobello Bks.
Dublin 20th August 1904

Sir,

I have the honour to forward
for your information and retention, a copy
of Agreement, together with Sketch Plan
and List of Fixtures of your letting No 1003
of No 11 Martello Tower, Sandycove.
Will you kindly acknowledge
receipt.

Yours faithfully

J. Blackwell
Lieut & Agent
D.O.R.E. South

Oliver Gogarty Esqr
No 11 Martello Tower
Sandy Cove

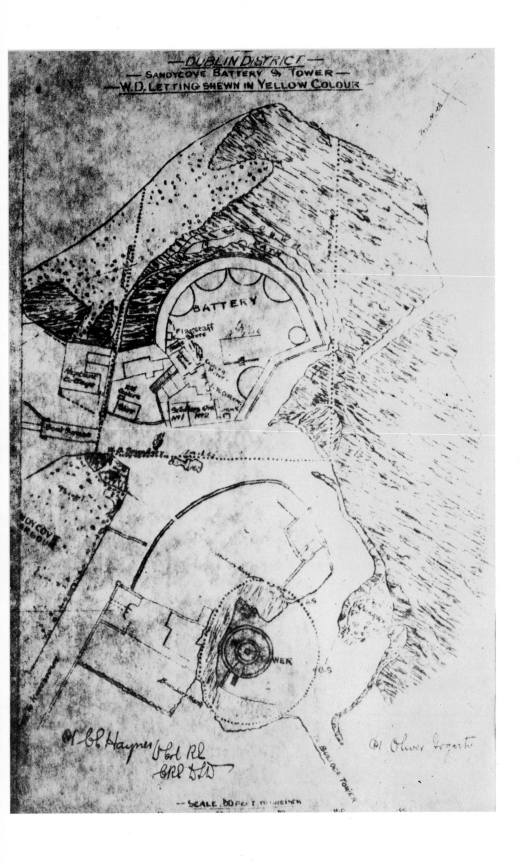